ANCIENT BELIEFS IN
THE IMMORTALITY
OF THE SOUL

WITH SOME ACCOUNT OF THEIR
INFLUENCE ON LATER VIEWS

BY
CLIFFORD HERSCHEL MOORE

COOPER SQUARE PUBLISHERS, INC.
NEW YORK
1963

Published 1963 by Cooper Square Publishers, Inc.
59 Fourth Avenue, New York 3, N. Y.
Library of Congress Catalog Card No. 63-10283

PRINTED IN THE UNITED STATES OF AMERICA

PREFACE

IN ANY historical discussion of man's belief in his existence beyond this earthly life it is necessary to recognize that at every known stage of human history, side by side with doubt and denial of any life beyond the grave, there has existed a great variety of concepts concerning the part of man that is to persist and the conditions of its persistence. On the nature of the " soul," its future powers and capacities, its abode, the duration of its future existence, and on a multitude of kindred topics, ordinary men have held and still hold the most divergent and the vaguest views; only theologians and philosophers attempt to form clear concepts on such difficult matters. Therefore the reader of the present essay will understand that the discussion ought not to be closely limited to ancient beliefs in the immortality of the soul, strictly speaking, but that every idea held in antiquity concerning the persistence of some part of man after death, whether for a limited period or for infinite time, may deserve a place so far as it has been influential on later thought; but the narrow limits of this book made it necessary to restrict its brief discussions to the most important doctrines. Moreover little attention has been given to ancient or modern denials of a life beyond the grave. Epicureanism, for example, important as it is in the history of thought, is briefly dismissed; and modern mechanistic views are omitted entirely.

Again, since it is impossible to determine what influence, if any, the views of India and Eastern Asia have had in the West in the past, I make no mention of them; furthermore, after the rupture between the East and the West, I have left the Eastern Church out of my account.

In the exposition of positive views it has seemed best to concentrate attention on certain great thinkers whose influence has been pre-eminent. It is comparatively easy to make the choice for antiquity; but the mediaeval period and modern times offer many difficulties. Hardly any two men will agree on the proper omissions; perhaps every reader will feel that some essential thinker has been neglected, and his feeling will probably be justified.

Although the earlier discussions deal somewhat with a variety of ancient views as to continuance after this life, whether for a time or forever, it has seemed better to limit the considerations of more modern beliefs in a future life to immortality proper, as defined by Kant in his *Critique of Practical Reason* (II. 2. 4) to the effect that the Immortality of the Soul means the infinitely prolonged existence and personality of one and the same rational being.

I wish to express my gratitude to the authorities of the British Museum and of the University of Cambridge for the privileges given me there; my obligations at home are too numerous to be recounted here in detail; yet I must make one exception, that I may thank my colleague, Professor Arthur Darby Nock, Frothingham professor of the History of Religion in Harvard University, for reading my manuscript and giving me valuable criticisms and suggestions.

C. H. M.

CONTENTS

[xi]

ANCIENT BELIEFS
IN THE IMMORTALITY OF
THE SOUL

Πείθεσθαι δ'ἐστὶ τῷ νομοθέτῃ χρεὼν τά τε ἄλλα καὶ λέγοντι ψυχὴν σώματος εἶναι τὸ πᾶν διαφέρουσαν, ἐν αὐτῷ τε τῷ βίῳ τὸ παρεχόμενον ἡμῶν ἕκαστον τοῦτ' εἶναι μηδὲν ἀλλ' ἢ τὴν ψυχήν, τὸ δὲ σῶμα ἰνδαλλόμενον ἡμῶν ἑκάστοις ἔπεσθαι, καὶ τελευτησάντων λέγεσθαι καλῶς εἴδωλα εἶναι τὰ τῶν νεκρῶν σώματα, τὸν δὲ ὄντα ἡμῶν ἕκαστον ὄντως, ἀθάνατον εἶναι ψυχὴν ἐπονομαζόμενον, παρὰ θεοὺς ἄλλους ἀπιέναι δώσοντα λόγον.

PLATO, *Laws*, XII, 959ab.

ANCIENT BELIEFS IN THE IMMORTALITY OF THE SOUL

I. HOMER. ORPHISM. ELEU-SINIAN MYSTERIES

A BELIEF that some part of man persists after death is well-nigh universal. In the Mediterranean area the scanty evidence that we have from the second millenium before our era, within the range of the Minoan-Mycenaean Age, seems to indicate that the ancestors of the later Greeks, or at least of their predecessors, whoever they may have been, gave tendance to their dead, or perhaps worshiped them; and it is probable that the Hellenic stocks, which later descended into the lands that they were to possess, brought similar practices with them, and continued the faithful service of their predecessors.[1]

Our earliest literary evidence is given us by the *Iliad* and *Odyssey*. The Homeric man did not doubt that ghostly images of mortals existed after death, insubstantial shades whose dreary lot held them beneath the earth, or kept them far out in the darkness by the stream of Oceanus, where Hades rules. Save for a few individuals there was no special punishment or reward for the deeds done in this life: the great majority of shades had no ethical recompense; nothing awaited them but a dull, cheerless existence which, compared with the joy and brightness of life on earth, was almost less than nothing. "Speak not lightly to me of death, glorious Odysseus. For so I might be on earth, I would rather be the servant of another, of a poor man who had little substance, than to be lord over all the dead." [2] Thus sadly spake to Odysseus the shade of god-like Achilles. The faint shadows of former men to the mind of the Homeric hero apparently had little power to bless or harm the living, who gave them scanty tendance and still less worship. It is true that in his passionate grief for his friend Patroclus, Achilles made great offerings at his funeral of honey and oil, horses, dogs, sheep, cattle, and twelve Trojan youths, while all the night he poured libations on the burning pyre. [3] Odysseus promised the shades that came gibbering to his magic draughts of blood, honey, milk, and wine and his offerings of barley grains, that when he had reached home he would sacrifice to them a barren cow.[4] But these are the only reminiscences in the epics of matters which were apparently of great concern in the age before Homer and which played a large part in the religious practices of later centuries. The Olympian religion tended to drive out or to obscure the worship of the dead. The nobles for whom Homer sang seem to have neglected or largely abandoned the ideas connected with such cults which, however, continued elsewhere and in other classes of society: indeed excavations have thus far shown that the tendance or worship of the departed was not the same in every locality or at all times.[5]

But in the sixth century our evidence as to beliefs in the continued existence of the soul after this life becomes more abundant. The cult of heroes, a class of *daemones* which includes chthonic divinities, great mortals of an earlier age, and according to some scholars " faded gods " of a remoter time, is widely attested. Certainly the second class just named owed its existence to the conviction that some mortals at least might put on immortality — a belief that ultimately found its baneful expression in the doctrine of the divinity of kings and in the practice of the apotheosis of emperors. But not the great alone might now hope for immortality; the ordinary man could attain that boon through sacrament and religious exercise.

By the seventh and sixth centuries before our era the Greek world had greatly changed from that society which is represented in the Homeric poems. Colonial expansion had widened men's thoughts; trade and industry had brought in wealth through the power of which a new aristocracy arose to dispute the ancient claims of birth. The city-state replaced the old tribal organization, while ancient custom lost its power before written constitutions. Many men began to claim a share in politics and society which their fathers had never dared demand; and more than this, in their new self-consciousness, they began to question the meaning of this world of men and gods, to ask whence they came and whither they were going. Philosophy arose; side by side with rationalism a mysticism developed and new religious ideas became prominent, which were of the greatest significance as touching the nature and destiny of the soul. The most important religious movement of this later time is that known as Orphism. Who Orpheus, its alleged founder, was we probably shall never know: he appears as a Thracian, a wonder-working musician, a priest of the god Dionysus: the founder of the Bacchic or Dionysiac mysteries. In any case the movement which bears his name was a development or a modification of the orgiastic rites of the Phrygio-Thracian Dionysus long known in Greek lands.

The ecstatic worship of this god, in which the devotee, spurred on by wild music and orgiastic dance, made unconscious of time or place, in frenzy tore living creatures asunder and devoured their raw flesh, was strangely foreign to the cult of the Olympians; but it offered an outlet to religious emotions which devotion to those staider gods could not give. Originally these Bacchic rites were probably intended to recall the dead god of vegetation back to life in the spring. The rebirth of such divinities has oftentimes become the warrant of man's hope of a renewed life for himself after his dead body, like the withered husks of grain, has been laid away to crumble into dust. Moreover through the wild Orphic ritual the devotee was "taken out of himself," his soul seemed for the time to be freed from the hampering body, to become one with the very god, so that the worshiper might claim for himself the divine name βάκχος. All this was religious intuition, devoid as yet of rational support; but in it lay implicit a belief in the dual nature of man — body and soul — the one of the earth mortal, the other divine; and it was natural to hope that, as the soul in its temporal freedom from the body enjoyed a divine life for the moment, so, when it should have finally departed from its present corporeal home, it would live forever with the god.

This intuitional belief or hope was supported by a sacred myth according to which man was sprung from the ashes of the Titans, those hostile powers whom Zeus had consumed with his thunderbolt as punishment for tearing in pieces and devouring the youthful god Dionysus. These ashes of the Titans still contained a divine spark of the god in the midst of their earthy matter: hence man's double nature — the soul divine, the body mortal and wicked. In this way the Dionysiac sectaries accounted for man's inner struggle: they perceived that he is both pulled by the baser motives of the flesh and prompted by the nobler aspirations of the soul. Their aim then was to purify the soul from the defilement of its corporeal home that in purity it might enjoy its proper life. This end might not be quickly accomplished: many rounds of life and death were needed before purification could be complete. While on earth man must follow a course of life marked by prohibitions of which the most important was that which forbade the eating of flesh and certain other foods; a ritual was developed with initiations, liturgies, and magic incantations for the purification and security of the devotee. In Hades the soul's lot was determined by its former life on earth: "They who are righteous beneath the rays of the sun, when they die have a gentler lot in a fair meadow by deep-flowing Acheron. But they who have worked wrong and insolence beneath the rays of the sun are led down beneath the watery plain of Cocytus into chill Tartarus." [6] According to a common belief, when a thousand years of joy or punishment had been passed in the abode of the dead, the soul was born again into a mortal body for a new sojourn on earth, which might indeed be spent in other than human form: "Wherefore

[9]

the changing soul of man, in the cycles of time, passes into various creatures: sometimes it is a horse, again it is a sheep, then a bird dread to see; again it takes the form of a dog with heavy voice, or as a chill snake creeps along the sacred earth." [7] Thus the soul passed from earth to Hades and back to earth again, each sojourn here or in the world below being a season of trial, punishment, and purification. Both realms rejected the most wicked, according to the philosopher-poet, Empedocles: "There is an oracle of Necessity, an ancient, eternal decree of the gods sealed with strong oaths: when one in sin stains his hands with murder, or when another joining in strife swears falsely, they become spirits who have long life as their portion, who are doomed to wander thrice ten thousand seasons far from the blessed, being born in the course of time into all forms of mortal creatures, shifting along life's hard paths. For the might of the air drives them to the sea and the sea spews them on the ground, and the land bares them to the rays of the bright sun, and the sun throws them in whirls of ether. One receives them from another, but all hate them. Of this number am even I now, an exile from God and a wanderer, for I put my trust in mad strife." [8]

What the ultimate fate of the wicked was to be, we have no clear knowledge — they may have been doomed to eternal rounds of existence, or to endless punishment in Hades; but we are told that in the Orphic hell the most horrible torments were inflicted on the sinful whose fate was no less fearful than the physical tortures of the damned in later Christian thought.

Those, however, who through successive reincarnations were finally purified, apparently left earth and Hades behind to live in freedom with the gods. On Orphic tablets discovered in Italy and Crete we find the triumphant soul joyfully addressing the gods: " I come from the pure. . . For I boast myself to be of your race. . . I have escaped from the sorrowful weary round, I have entered with eager feet the ring desired. I have passed to the bosom of the mistress queen of the lower world." In answer comes the assurance: "O happy and blessed one, thou shalt be god instead of mortal." [9]

Certain significant facts are clear from this brief exposition. The Homeric hero regarded this world as his most desirable abode; the Orphic devotee turned his gaze to the world beyond and thought his earthly life was of moment only as one stage toward a future life in which he was to realize his complete happiness; he felt that his mortal body was a hampering, sinful thing, but that his soul was divine and hence immortal. His ultimate happiness depended on purity from sin. Thus a powerful moral motive was introduced into Greek thought, a motive which was to be of the greatest ethical consequence.

Orphic ideas were shared in no small part by the Pythagoreans; they spread to many parts of Greece, degenerating in the hands of charlatans, who offered salvation to all who would resort to their magic initiations and ritual, or supplying the nobler spirits with inspiration and a higher course of life. We cannot now tell what proportion of the people was affected by these ideas. At the best the Orphic confidence in the immortality of the soul rested only on an intuition; it was simply an emotional belief, parallel in a way to the hope cherished by those initiated in the mysteries at Eleusis.

The Eleusinian mysteries, celebrated from

an unknown antiquity, had reached a developed form as early as the seventh century before our era; they continued to be practised until A.D. 396, when Alaric the Goth destroyed the sanctuary at Eleusis. In these mysteries life after death was taken for granted: there was no argument adduced to support that belief. Those who had been initiated into the rites of Demeter were assured a happy life hereafter, while the uninitiate were doomed to a sad fate in the house of Hades. Thus here the means by which joy and security were to be obtained were ritualistic; and, in accord with a certain habit of the human mind, confidence in the efficacy of the ritual persistently remained the initiates' chief assurance to the end, although by the fifth century before our era a moral significance had been given the rites.[10]

It is impossible, however, to determine how widespread beliefs in a life after death were among the great mass of the Greek people in antiquity. Grave monuments usually show us scenes from this life rather than give us glimpses of a world beyond; sepulchral inscriptions down to the middle of the fifth century are silent as to a future existence; after that date we occasionally find an expression of hope or confidence in a posthumous life. Yet silence cannot be taken as proof that the relatives of the dead had no belief in the soul's continuance; nor need we take the flippant epigrams or cynical declarations of a later age as warrants for the thoughts of all men. In fact there probably existed among the ancients every variety of belief and doubt that can be found in latter times.[11] Certain it is that the widespread expectation of an existence beyond the grave and the passionate desire for future security that prevailed in the Hellenistic and Roman periods were rooted in ancient hope and confidence. New ideas as to the nature of the soul and the place of its abode hereafter, new impulses to hope, and new concepts of reward and punishment arose with the passing of the centuries; but on the whole the history of Greek belief in some kind of a future life is probably unbroken even from pre-Hellenic centuries.

II. PLATO. ARISTOTLE

IT WAS during the latter half of the fifth century before our era that philosophy took up her abode in Athens. In the intellectual ferment that accompanied the disasters of the Peloponnesian War attention was turned to a consideration of man's relation to his fellows and of his place in the universe by the speculations of the Sophists and above all by the persistent questionings of Socrates whose greatest follower, Plato, was destined to exert a mighty and lasting influence on human thought and belief. Before him, as we have already seen, confidence in the continued existence of the soul after death was based on religious hope and intuition: it remained for the founder of the Academy to give that confidence a rational basis, or at least a basis that supported human longings with comforting and assuring arguments.

In the *Phaedo*, which reports the conversation of Socrates with his friends on the day of his death, the master is represented as cheering his sorrowing companions with arguments to prove that the true philosopher is a man who recognizes that he is a " chattel " of God, and who therefore is ready to die whenever it is God's will; for Socrates is confident that the good and wise gods to whom man belongs and who watch over him here will not fail to care for him after death. Such is the faith that encourages him to face death not only calmly, but with the hope that after this life he may enjoy the company of the best who have gone before him: that is, he believes that the life after death for the true philosopher will be better than this mundane existence. His confidence in a happy hereafter for the good and wise therefore is based first of all on his faith in the goodness of the Divine — the faith in which he has lived, and which he will not now give up in the face of death, for to do so would be to prove false to all his past.

The true philosopher, according to Socrates, is in fact engaged in nothing else but the " practice " of dying, the " rehearsal " of being dead; for the soul in this life, being constantly enslaved by the desires and weaknesses of the body, is prevented from perceiving the true nature of anything and from grasping the truth:

if therefore a man is ever to know anything absolutely, his soul must be freed from the do-
minion of the body that he may see the actual
realities with its eyes alone. Lovers of knowledge then will strive to avoid association and
communion with the body so far as possible,
keeping themselves pure from it until God himself shall set them free, for only so may they
perhaps know the truth here on earth and be
prepared to grasp it fully when the soul shall
be wholly freed from its corporeal home. This
is what the true philosophers mean by the
" practice " of dying, for they endeavor, so far
as in them lies, to keep the soul pure from the
body in this life that they may now have in
some degree the vision of that which they shall
clearly see when the soul is freed by death.
Therefore the lover of knowledge does not
fear to die. But common men cannot understand that attitude.[12]

Thus far in their discourse the immortality
of the soul has been taken for granted, but now
the friends of Socrates desire reasons for believing that it is so. The first argument that
the master offers is based on the doctrine of
" opposites," which was a commonplace of
early Greek speculation on physical questions.

According to it we observe everywhere opposites — greater and smaller, better and worse, stronger and weaker, more just and unjust, etc. A man becomes stronger by becoming less weak, and so on: that is, opposites come out of opposites. This principle, Socrates argues must apply to life and death: the dead comes from the living and the living from the dead; and this conclusion accords with common observation; for we are all familiar with the phenomenon of dying, which is changing from life, and we must believe that "becoming alive" is actually "becoming the opposite of dying," and therefore that life comes from death. So Socrates finds support for the "ancient tale" that he remembers, which says that when men die they go to Hades, and then after a time return to earth. This is none other than the Orphic doctrine of rebirths long current in Greek thought and known even to the unlettered. But this belief presupposes that the soul survives the vicissitudes of the body.[13]

At this point the Theban Cebes interrupts to say that that same conclusion might have been reached by using the master's own familiar argument that all learning is only the recollection of something known before. But a second disciple, Simmias, declares that he does not recall that argument very well and begs Socrates to give them the proofs that they may understand. So Socrates complies and says that if by proper questioning we can secure from even an ignorant man the correct solution of a problem, it must be that the man has simply had the truth " recalled to him," that he has been " reminded " of something that he has known before. This may be most easily perceived in connection with geometry.[14] Therefore we can understand that there is such a thing as absolute equality, although we can never perceive through the senses that any two objects are exactly equal, but only that they are approximately equal; yet this approximate relation of which our senses tell us " reminds " us that perfect equality exists in itself: it is through this concept of ideal equality that we are able to estimate approximate equality. The same is true of beauty, goodness, justice, holiness, and all other essences or ideals. But we could not be reminded of ideal equality by approximate equality unless we already knew what the ideal was; and since we cannot imagine that we have acquired these ideal concepts, or have gained this knowledge of absolute truths at birth, there is but one conclusion left us, or as Socrates puts the matter: " Then may we not say, Simmias, that if, as we are always repeating, there is an absolute beauty, and goodness, and an absolute essence of all things; and if to this, which is now discovered to have existed in our former state, we refer all our sensations and with this compare them, does it not necessarily follow that as these absolute essences exist, so our souls have had an existence before we were born; but if these absolutes do not exist, there would be no force in the argument? And must it not equally follow that the ideas do exist and that our souls also had an existence before we were born; and that if these ideas do not exist, our souls did not exist either." [15]

Although Simmias and Cebes readily grant that the pre-existence of the soul is sufficiently established, they still feel that this does not prove that the soul is immortal and naturally desire to hear further on this point. In answer Socrates suggests that if they accept the earlier argument based on opposites, the continued existence of the soul need not be doubted. But to still all childish fears he proceeds to argue that the soul is of the same simple and unchanging nature as the ideas; being uncompounded it will not change or vary as do things which we perceive through the senses — such things as men, or horses, or clothes. Moreover the soul is naturally the ruler and governor of the body; but to govern is a function of the divine. Now since the soul resembles the divine, indeed is the very likeness of the divine, the immortal, the intelligible, the uniform, the indissoluble, and the unchangeable, while the body is closely akin to every opposite of the soul's nature, the soul must be naturally eternal, and on her departure from the body, if she has kept herself free from pollution, must go to a life of bliss, to the company of the gods. But if a soul, falsifying her true nature, has been enamored of the body and has been polluted by sensual joys, then she must pay the penalty by a cycle of rebirths. Only the soul that loves wisdom can attain to divinity, that is, to immortality.

We need not pause now to enlarge upon the ethical doctrine here set forth: in a word it is that the soul which has been concerned with things that are eternal rather than the things that are temporal and changing, must thereby become itself eternal, that is, divine, immortal.

Obviously this doctrine is far more than the familiar doctrine of the indissolubility of "a simple substance," for here the soul's happiness depends on its devotion to the noblest purposes, to wisdom.

Yet Simmias and Cebes are not wholly satisfied: the former feels that from Socrates's argument concerning the soul and the body, it may well be that the soul is the "harmony" of the body; and that just as the harmony of the lyre, which is incorporeal and invisible, can hardly be said to exist when the strings of the lyre are loosed or the instrument is broken, so it may be that the soul ceases to exist when the body is broken up. Cebes for his part cannot see that anything has been proved beyond the pre-existence of the soul. Granting that the soul is stronger than the body, like a weaver making a succession of cloaks, the soul may make and wear out a number of bodies and in the process it may itself grow old like the weaver, become exhausted, and die.

Socrates alone is undismayed by these serious objections. He first warns his friends against a hatred of ideas, a lack of faith in arguments, which may arise from ignorance of the art of reasoning; then he quickly removes the objection that Simmias has raised by pointing out that if the soul is the harmony of the body it cannot have existed before the body. But Simmias is convinced by the doctrine of recollection that it does exist before it is incorporated in man's visible frame. Next Socrates turns to Cebes, whose fear that the soul may wear out her energy and cease to be is a more serious matter, as the modern mechanistic interpretation of nature shows. First Socrates acquaints his friends with the course of his own studies and development. When a young man he was greatly given, he says, to the study of the natural sciences, and earnestly examined the teachings of the earlier philosophers and men of science from the Milesians to Anaxagoras, only in the end to be left in complete disappointment and doubt. Then he fell back on that method of reasoning which is familiar in mathematics, wherein we investigate truth by making postulates or propositions, which we then test by examining the consequences. If the consequences of a postulate are found to correspond with facts we may regard it as true. So he came to postulate the existence of absolute beauty, goodness, greatness, and the like; by partaking of these absolutes, individual things become beautiful, or good, or great. These are the real "forms," the "ideas," which are permanent and unchanging.

All his listeners having now assented to his method of argument and to its conclusions, Socrates proceeds to the most convincing proof of the soul's immortality. By apt illustrations he shows that no "form" can ever unite with the opposite "form": we may, for example, not say of Simmias that he possesses both "greatness" and "smallness" of stature, but only that he is taller than Socrates and shorter than Phaedo; nor can we maintain that the integer three participates at once in the form "odd" and the opposite form "even." The "even" cannot enter into three, for if it could it would cause the "odd" to retreat: the very nature of the integer would be completely changed and we should have in its place an even number, say two; or else the "odd" would maintain itself and the integer three would be unchanged. No number can be odd and even at the same time. Thus forms are seen to be essentials of the objects under discussion. But life is an essential of the soul: it is alive and brings life to any body in which it dwells. It cannot admit the opposite of life, that is, death.

Therefore the soul is imperishable; but that which does not perish is immortal. So we must believe that when the body dies the soul does not cease to be, but rather withdraws to some other place.

We must not think that Plato was convinced of the perfect validity of these arguments. To his master and to him alike, a belief in immortality seems to have been in the end an act of faith which they supported by persuasive reasoning. In the *Phaedo* Socrates proceeds to turn his arguments to the practical bearing that a belief or faith in the soul's immortality has on the conduct of life: if we once admit that a confidence in the immortal nature of the soul is not irrational, the "tendance of the soul" is obviously man's greatest interest, for on the character that his soul carries over into the next world will depend its happiness or its sorrow.[16] This, however, is not the place to enlarge on Plato's cogent ethics. We must rather return to a third and more convincing argument.

In the *Phaedrus* Socrates reasons thus: "Every soul is immortal, for that which is ever in motion is immortal; but that which moves another and is moved by another, in ceasing to

[25]

move ceases to live. Only the self-moving, since it never leaves itself, never ceases to move; but this is also the source and beginning of motion to all that moves besides. The beginning, however, is unbegotten, for everything that is begotten must have a beginning, yet the beginning is not begotten of anything; for if the beginning were begotten of anything, it would not be a beginning, and since it is not begotten, it must also be indestructible. Thus that which moves itself must be the beginning of motion; and this can be neither destroyed nor begotten. But since that which is moved by itself has been seen to be immortal, he who says that this self-motion is the essence and the very idea of the soul, will not be put to shame." [17]

It is clear that whenever Plato (or Socrates) discusses the soul in connection with the immaterial " forms," the " ideas," which are at once the cause of all things and the bases of all reality, he shows or assumes that these " ideas " are known to us only through the reason. The senses can perceive nothing but corporeal things, the transient material objects of the sensuous world; it is the intellect that apprehends the invisible realities. But these

[26]

real " forms " are eternal, and it must be that man's reason, by which alone they can be apprehended, is of the same nature, or it could have no knowledge of them: accordingly the reasoning soul must be eternal, immortal, knowing neither creation nor death.

Whether Plato believed that the individual souls retained their individuality after death has been a matter of dispute among the learned. Nowhere does he explicitly state his views on this point, but it is somewhat hard to understand his emphasis on the individual, his numerous arguments to establish the immortality of the individual soul, and the implications contained in his ethical discussions, without thinking that he took it for granted that the individual soul was eternal.[18] Yet it is important to keep in mind that the Greeks laid less stress on the survival of individual consciousness than Christians have been inclined to do, and that when Greek philosophers speak of the soul as being eternal they do not always interpret " eternity " to be an " endless continuation of time," as is commonly done by careless thinkers.

As we have already seen, the Orphics and their philosophic brothers, the Pythagoreans, apparently were the first among the Greeks to conceive of life after death primarily as a retributive state in which rewards and punishments are to be meted out according to the soul's deserts; nor was it to their minds in Hades alone that the soul suffered or enjoyed its just recompense, for its successive incarnations were also periods of retribution and purification until the rounds of existence were accomplished and the soul entered into its final state. It has also been shown how Plato too accepted the doctrine of palingenesis and retributive justice here and in Hades, securing thereby a powerful ethical argument: only the soul of the true philosopher who thinks that it must accept the deliverance from the bondage of the body that philosophy offers and to the extent of its powers abstains from sensual pleasures, desires, pains, and fears, may secure release after three rebirths, provided that soul has each time chosen a higher life. Then the soul shall be free and may depart to dwell with the gods.[19]

Thus as early as the sixth century at least, men had passed from the idea of mere continuance after death to a belief in rewards and punishments hereafter for the deeds done in the flesh. Undoubtedly the Orphics, like a considerable proportion of men in all ages, including the present, conceived of very carnal and earthly rewards in that unearthly future existence — notions which called forth Plato's scorn and ridicule. To him the recompense of virtue was to be found in becoming like God, so far as possible. This he counted the greatest reward that reasoning man can receive or desire.[20] This he felt to be a great religious truth, not absolutely demonstrated by intellectual processes, but a noble faith and a high conviction of supreme significance for the conduct of life, since under its impulse man ever sought for real virtue, living justly and dying bravely. So great an impression have Plato's convictions made on men that their influence on later thinkers, ethical and religious, has been and still is profound.

Plato was by nature a poet, with a deep strain of religious mysticism in his nature. He starts with the concept of the soul as something apart from the body, belonging to a different world from that of the body, and therefore pre-existent and independent. Hence his thoroughgoing dualism which causes him to treat body and soul as distinct entities, although in what we call human life they appear in combination. This duality of soul and body was parallel to his doctrine of " forms " of " ideas," to which we have already referred. According to this doctrine there exists behind this transient and multiform world of phenomena known to us through our senses a real and permanent world of " forms," " ideas," which can be apprehended only by reason. The " forms " are the eternal realities, and the individual object perceived by us owes its existence solely to the fact that matter has "partaken" of the " form " whereby it has secured its temporary existence. We may best use Plato's own homely illustrations from the beginning of the tenth book of the *Republic,* where Socrates and Glaucon are conversing. There Glaucon readily agrees to his master's proposition that although there are many beds and tables in the world, there are only two " ideas " or " forms," one of bed, the other of table. The carpenter makes us a bed or a table by working his material in accordance with the " idea " of bed or table, by causing matter to " partake " of the " form," the " idea." The individual table or bed therefore is only a transient copy of the reality, that is, of the " idea " or " form," by sharing in which it gains its own temporal existence. These illustrations, although Plato's own, if taken by themselves, may readily be misleading, for they explain the nature of only material individual things such as we see about us every day. But, as we have seen above, Plato's doctrine of "ideas," "forms," is thorough-going and holds as strongly for what we call the abstract as for the sensible world: the righteous man is good because he partakes of the idea of goodness, the beautiful statue is beautiful in so far as it partakes of the idea of beauty, and so on through the whole range. This world of "ideas," of "forms," alone has real existence, and it exists quite apart from the phenomenal world; the latter comes into being only through sharing in the real world of "forms," which exist in the mind of God. Plato holds thus to a thorough-going dualism: in the macrocosm the phenomenal world is set over against the ideal world, in the microcosm man's material body is contrasted with the immortal soul.

PLATO started with a religious presupposition, and then proceeded to develop his teachings with special reference to religion and ethics.

His greatest pupil Aristotle, however, looked upon the world from the biological point of view and endeavored to interpret the soul from his observation of the living organism.

Employing the same wide freedom that earlier philosophers exhibited in the use of the Greek word *psyche,* "soul," Aristotle defined the "soul" as the principle of life; and as he made a distinction between three levels of living beings — vegetable, animal, and man — so he recognized three grades of psychical activity or function. All living beings of every sort depend upon nutritive or assimilative functions and are subject to growth and decay; so that, according to the Stagirite, we must recognize in all living creatures, from the lowest to the highest, the presence of a nutritive element (τὸ θρεπτικόν) or soul (ἡ θρεπτικὴ ψυχή) by virtue of which all things possess life. In contrast to vegetable organisms, all animals possess sensation (τὸ αἰσθητικόν) and consequently appetency — they feel pleasure and pain, they are prompted by desire and dislike. Therefore we must recognize in all animals an "appetitive soul" (τὸ ὀρεκτικόν) which accompanies the "nutritive" soul. But man, and any other being that may be superior

to him, has the power of thinking (τὸ διανοη-
τικόν) and intellect (νοῦς). This intellect,
peculiar to man and possible higher beings,
is at once active (τὸ ποιοῦν) and passive
(τὸ δεκτικόν): the latter element is the potential
element of the mind — it must be receptive
(τὸ πάσχον) of the object of thought, just as
the senses are receptive of impressions from
sensible objects; through the active element
the potentiality becomes an actuality and
thinking then results. The soul in this sense
Aristotle maintains has been well called the
"place of forms or ideas"; but he continues, "the part of the soul which we call intellect is nothing at all before it thinks." The
active element in the soul he holds is always
in action; and that on this activity depends
all reasoning. This part of the soul is for him
"alone immortal and eternal" (ἀθάνατον καὶ
ἀΐδιον).[21]

In thus allowing that the active reason is
immortal and eternal Aristotle is clearly in-
consistent, for his argument up to this point
is that soul and body are inseparable, the soul
being the soul of its peculiar body, the cor-
relative relation of soul and body being similar
to that of form and matter; and as form is

never found apart from matter or matter without form, both being necessary for the existence of the concrete individual object, so, he has argued, soul and body together make up the individual man: we never know them apart. The body is the potentiality, the soul the "actuality" or "fulfillment" ($\dot{\epsilon}\nu\tau\epsilon\lambda\dot{\epsilon}\chi\epsilon\iota\alpha$), by which the potentiality is realized. Hence we are surprised when we find that he sets apart the "active reason" from all the lower grades of the soul and predicates for it immortality. We cannot now say with certainty why he does this, but in a passage where he is discussing the divisibility of the vegetative soul he prepares his readers for the division of the intellect, for he points out that the fact that plants can be "slipped" and each slip live, shows that the vegetative soul can be divided, or else is plural; worms likewise can be cut without destroying life or sensation and movement in the several sections. And then he continues: " But as regards intellect ($\nu o \hat{v} s$) and the speculative faculty ($\dot{\eta}\ \theta\epsilon\omega\rho\eta\tau\iota\kappa\dot{\eta}$ $\delta\dot{v}\nu\alpha\mu\iota s$) the case is not yet clear. This speculative faculty would seem, however, to be a distinct species of the soul, and it alone is capable of separation from the body, as that which is eternal (τὸ ἀΐδιον) from that which is perishable."

Again in comparing the potentiality of the intellect (νοῦς) for thought to the potentiality of the senses for perception, he observes that there is a fundamental difference between the intellect and the senses in that the latter are dependent on the body, so that, for example, we lose the sense of hearing when our ears are dulled by too loud noise and sight when our eyes are dazed by too intense light; whereas the intellect when it has been thinking on an object of intense thought is not less, but even more able to think of inferior objects. Hence he concludes that the intellect is separable from the body.[22]

Interpreters, ancient and modern, have disputed much over Aristotle's meaning here, and have speculated long over what he conceived the ultimate state of the "immortal" and "eternal" part of the soul to be. Certain it is that he held that this part of the soul when disembodied has no memory of the body in which it once dwelt. The faculty of memory he assigned to the passive part of the intellect, which is perishable. Did he then think of the immortal reason as an eternal entity, existing without self-consciousness, or did he identify active intelligence with God, who in the *Metaphysics* is described as " the source of intelligibility in all intelligibles " ? Many with good cause have held the latter view to be the most probable; and in any case Aristotle certainly regarded the active soul as similar to God if not identical with Him. But it could have no memory, no individuality, and therefore no conscious life apart from the human body accompanying its earthly existence.[23] More than this we cannot say with confidence.

III. STOICISM. NEOPLATONISM

THE GREAT idealistic and spiritual-
istic masters were soon followed by
two materialists, Zeno, the founder of
Stoicism, and Epicurus, the father of the school
that bears his name. The former had listened
to Cynic, Megarian, and Platonic teachers, so
that his philosophy naturally had an eclectic
character. Moreover men's thoughts had been
profoundly influenced by the changes that took
place in the fourth century before our era.
With the rise of Macedon the political freedom
of the tiny Greek city-states was curtailed or
lost: the individual had no longer an oppor-
tunity for that unhampered political life which
formerly, in the Greek democracies at least,
had given men abundant chance for activity in
an effort to realize their desires and ambitions
in a sphere outside themselves. Consequently
they were now turned inward and forced to
draw their satisfaction from an internal discipline that should make their will superior to
all that external fortune and circumstance

could marshal against it. Furthermore, the decay of national life within the city-state loosened the bonds of local attachment and developed in society at the same time a new individualism and a new cosmopolitanism. This latter characteristic was favored by that sudden expansion of the political horizon which Alexander's conquests in three continents produced.

A rapid readjustment of thought and attitude was necessary in this new world where the great mass of men could no longer find their satisfactions in external action, but were compelled to fortify themselves within their own souls. A vigorous and defensive ethical discipline was, therefore, the main interest of Stoicism from the first, and the need of this discipline was not lessened when the teachings of the Porch were adopted by the Romans as the decaying Republic passed into the Empire, which at its best gave little genuine liberty to the individual.

The aim of the Stoic school from the first was to train the individual to be superior to all external affects, to rise above all passions into a state of freedom ($\dot{a}\pi\dot{a}\theta\epsilon\iota a$) which should make him captain of his soul. By the first century of our era Stoicism had become almost exclusively a philosophy of religious edification; but it is necessary to consider for a moment its physics, under which the Stoics included theology and cosmology, to understand its doctrine touching the nature and the fate of the soul.

In their theory as to the nature of the universe, the Stoics had resorted to a materialism which they drew from the teachings of the earlier Greek materialists, according to whom matter alone existed. But with this materialistic monism they combined a doctrine, possibly taken from Aristotle, according to which they saw two aspects or principles in matter, the one active, forming and directing, and the other passive, being formed and directed. The rôle of this latter corresponded to that of matter in Aristotle's system, while the active principle included his efficient, formal, and final causes, or as we may say — intelligence, mind, or soul.[24] The soul then for them was a mode or function of matter: consequently it was to be regarded as material no less than the stones, wood, and other objects that are universally recognized as matter; but they thought it to be composed of the finest possible particles such as are found in currents of air or in fire; and therefore they not only used these two illustrations, especially that of fire, to explain the intelligent soul, but they frequently identified the soul with them; and their doctrine that matter was interpenetrable made it easy for them to believe that a finer matter could penetrate and perfectly combine with a coarser. This material intelligence they held to be immanent in all matter, and since the cosmos is a unified whole, the intelligence that permeates it, moves, and directs it is the World-soul. In the same way every living microcosm has its soul, not distinct from the World-soul, but a particle of it, or in the striking phrase of Epictetus, it is a fragment of God.[25]

In sharp contrast to the views of Aristotle and his immediate successors, who held that the present cosmos was eternal, the early Stoics maintained that the universe would, from time to time, be consumed in fire, and that then a new order of creation would begin and the cycle would once more be repeated. Some allowed a limited existence to men's souls after the death of the body, Cleanthes to the souls of all, Chrysippus only to those of the wise, until the next cosmic conflagration, when apparently the individual souls would be reabsorbed into the World-soul, that universal animating fire.

Within two centuries from its birth, Stoicism had become eclectic, and at least two eminent teachers, Panaetius, who may be called the Stoic apostle to the Romans in the second century before our era, and his pupil Posidonius (*c.* 130–46 B.C.), the friend and teacher of such men as Marius, Pompey, and Cicero, modified the earlier doctrines with great freedom. The former abandoned the cyclical theory of the world with its periodic destructions and recreations of the cosmos, and refused to allow the souls of even the wise an individual existence for a limited period after corporeal death. Posidonius reverted to the theory of world-cycles, but differed greatly from the earlier leaders in his psychological views; under Platonic influence he was led to believe even in the pre-existence and immortality of the soul. Such an attitude, however, was exceptional among even the later Stoics. Seneca can offer no confident arguments for immortality, but he does express a hope so eager that men once thought he must have been a Christian. The truth is that before the beginning of our era most Stoics had lost their interest in speculations as to the nature of the other world, and ordinarily concentrated their thought on the problem of living according to reason in this. Therefore the Stoic views as to the continued existence of the soul after death cease to be of much concern to us in our present discussion.

The Epicureans also, with their complete materialism, may be dismissed in the briefest manner, for they held that the soul had no life apart from the body to which it belonged: it came into existence at the moment of conception and was dissolved at death, its fine atoms, like the grosser ones of the body, being dissipated until some later time when they should become parts of new souls in other bodies.[26]

It is rather in those philosophies which were largely based on Platonism and Pythagoreanism that we must look for hopes of immortality for the human soul. During the first two centuries of our era, many thinkers followed eclectic courses of thought in which the two schools just named had the larger shares. They prepared the way for the extreme transcendence of that revived Platonism which was to be the last contribution of the ancient world to philosophical thought and mysticism.

In the second century of our era there was a reaction toward metaphysical and theological thinking away from that devotion to practical ethics that had so fully occupied the attention during the previous four or five centuries. With regard to the immortality of the soul, the majority probably inclined toward Plato's views; yet Galen, the famous teacher of medicine (A.D. 131–c. 200), was cautious even to the extent of leaving the question of the incorporeality of the soul undecided — an attitude of mind which was perhaps natural to a physician. But three generations earlier Plutarch and many others held firmly to a belief in immortality, as Philo the Jew had maintained that the soul by its very nature is immortal; but Philo also taught that a wicked life can destroy the soul, while it is righteousness which wins a happy immortality.[27]

The last great system of Greek philosophy is Neoplatonism, which is at once the summation and the climax of eight centuries of Hellenic speculation; and it accurately represents that longing for tranquillity in this life, for a revelation of God, and for the assurance of future happiness that prevailed in the Greco-Roman world from the close of the fourth century before our era. This final ancient philosophy was initiated at Alexandria, the peculiar meeting place of Jewish and Hellenic thought, by Ammonius Saccas at the beginning of the third Christian century. Its most famous representatives were Origen, the Church father, and Plotinus. As its name implies it was largely based on Platonism with which were combined many borrowings from other schools. Like its immediate predecessors it held to the transcendence of God, between whom and this created world stand intermediate powers, emanations from God, whose activity is constant but not exercised directly in creation. God himself has no form ($\mu o \rho \phi \acute{\eta}$) or figure ($\imath \delta \acute{\epsilon} a$); he is not comprehensible by reason, but is above all reason and all knowledge. He abides neither in time nor in place; he is absolute unity, the first cause and the final cause alike. As the sun sends its rays in every direction without effort or loss, so God emanates Intelligence ($\nu o \hat{\upsilon} s$), wherein are immanent the Ideas which cause all things to come into existence. The second grade of emanation is the World-soul ($\psi \upsilon \chi \acute{\eta}$) which in its turn embraces all individual souls. The World-soul stands midway between the intelligible and the phenomenal worlds. The individual souls are not separate parts of the universal soul, but nevertheless there is a multiplicity of them. When they are incorporated in separate bodies we may properly speak of them as individual souls, for each soul in its intellectual part is universal and at the same time individual.[28]

Of the inherent difficulty in such a concept as this, Plotinus is well aware: he argues that quantity and space, which are categories belonging to material things, have no application to immaterial souls. The figure of light emanating from the sun and illuminating material objects, without being separated from the whole, is his clearest illustration of his concept of this difficult matter. It is true that he holds that in a certain sense we must distinguish two grades in the soul itself: in so far as it is intelligence, it is indivisible, but its lower nature can be divided so that the parts have a separate existence.

The individual souls descend into matter which they pervade and shape, imparting to the beings thus created life, sensation, and reason; yet under the baneful influence of matter, the souls of men sometimes forget their divine origin, even as the sunlight is dimmed or lost by its descent into darkness; like rebellious children, such souls reject their father, abandon their own nature which would lead them only to seek the honorable, and thus fall ever deeper into sin. Therefore the sinner must be turned from his ways by a noble discipline and recalled to the things that belong to the soul.[29] Not all can rise above the senses, but the majority continue to identify the good with pleasure and the evil with pain; some better souls, however, are able to devote themselves to the practical virtues; while a few rare spirits, endowed with greater strength and clearer vision than the mass, may rise above the clouds and mists of this world into the clear light of the world above, like men returning to their native city after long wanderings. The soul's aim is likeness to God: in the contemplative life, man's highest activity, in which he is concerned with intelligence alone, he becomes himself divine.[30]

For those few who thus through contemplation attain to divinity, there is a further possibility: their souls may be allowed in ecstasy, forgetting self and thought alike, to rise to complete knowledge of God and to unity with him. Thus at once, while yet associated with the body, such rare souls may attain at moments all that the Beatific Vision of the Christian Church has ever vouchsafed the spirits of its saints in heaven. Such sight and knowledge we are told Plotinus had been given four times during the six years that his pupil Porphyry had been with him; while Porphyry himself had once enjoyed the Vision.[31]

Of the immortality of the soul Plotinus could have no doubts. For him the soul is eternal, indestructible, the very principle of life; it has the power to see the pure and eternal realities so it may even mount upward from this transient, temporal home and see God himself. It therefore cannot die. So long as the human soul is in the body it exercises many functions like sensation, memory, opinion, and reasoning which are necessary in the sensible world; but when it is freed from the body these activities become latent, for they are superfluous. Whether the disembodied soul was thought to retain its individuality is not clear. Plotinus certainly regards separation, individuality as imperfection, and in one place he says that the soul yonder is undifferentiated and undivided (ψυχὴ ἐκεῖ ἀδιάκριτος καὶ ἀμέριστος). Yet he recognizes plurality as existent in the One, in God, and he seems to regard souls as distinct entities. There is not necessarily a contradiction here, for individuals may lie latent in the One and the disembodied souls be absorbed into the universal soul.[32]

In all discussion of the retention of individuality in the other life we must guard against falling into those errors to which we are easily led by the common and somewhat superficial fear of losing one's self if individuality is not preserved. Separateness is imperfection and belongs to time: only in complete unity is perfection attained, and therefore the retention of individuality in eternity is not a thing to be aimed at or indeed possible. At least such is apparently the view of Plotinus. Needless to say he never falls so low as to regard mundane joys as the proper rewards for virtue, or corporeal pains as punishments due sin. For unrighteousness souls may be condemned to live on in other bodies, and disembodied souls may be afflicted by demons or aided by guardian angels. But punishments and rewards are not of a carnal nature.[33]

The attitude of Plotinus toward the question of the retention of individuality is on the whole in accord with the thought of his predecessors, for while Plato may have conceived of personality as persistent, his position is by no means clear; and all other masters lay no store on the survival of the conscious self; yet there are indications that popular Neoplatonism regarded individual survival as important. Personal conscious immortality was apparently believed in by the Orphics, but in philosophy and theology proper it was first regarded as indispensable by the Christians.

Before we consider the Christian views of immortality in their relation to the doctrines developed by peculiarly Greek thought it will be well to summarize the results of that historic development which we have thus far been considering.

First we must note the dualistic view of man which had become so firmly established that even such monistic systems as Stoicism and Epicureanism, with their theoretically complete materialism, could not escape its influence. Apparently the Orphics and the Pythagoreans were the first clearly to conceive of man as a double being, made up of body and soul: the body is then the temporary dwelling-place of the soul which cometh from afar. Moreover the body was regarded by them as base and evil while the soul was by nature divine and noble; but it had been degraded by association with the body, so that man's aim and hope was to free his divine element from its baneful, sensuous habitation that at last it might enter into its immortal bliss. In Plato's hands this " ancient tale " was ennobled into a powerful ethical argument and the older intuitive hope of immortality was supported by appealing proofs. Parallel to this anthropological dualism was the concept of the entire sensuous world as base and evil, while the supersensuous was divine and perfect. At the same time in the Platonic psychology a distinction was made between the nobler part of the soul, its reasoning part ($\tau\grave{o}$ $\lambda o\gamma\iota\sigma\tau\iota\kappa\acute{o}\nu$) on the one hand, and the lower parts, the appetitive ($\tau\grave{o}$ $\dot{\epsilon}\pi\iota\theta\upsilon\mu\eta\tau\iota\kappa\acute{o}\nu$) and the courageous ($\tau\grave{o}$ $\theta\upsilon\mu o\epsilon\iota\delta\acute{\epsilon}s$), on the other. As was stated earlier, only the reasoning part is held by Plato in his later dialogues to be immortal. Similarly Aristotle endows the active intellect alone with immortality, while all other parts of the soul die with the body. Thus the two great masters of the fourth century added to the anthropological dualism which they had inherited, a psychological distinction between the immortal part of the soul and those parts that ceased with the body.

Again in the Hellenistic and Roman periods in which political and social disasters culminated in the loss of freedom and the formation of the Roman Empire, to be succeeded by economic decay which diminished even sensuous satisfactions, men's thoughts were turned from the joys which this world could no longer give, to seek salvation first in an ethical discipline which looked to the development of the will that men might find their rewards and safety in the realm of reason, in the supersensuous world. The chief philosophic trend from 300 B.C. on is a religious one, prompted by the desire for the security of the soul. In these circumstances it was inevitable that Platonism with its attractive and nobly ascetic discipline should play the largest part. Here too the Stoic school made most important contributions to practice. Yet the Greek passion for knowledge could not be satisfied with ethical discipline alone, and gradually there grew up a sense of the inadequacy of man's unaided effort: by himself he could not attain that certain knowledge which alone would satisfy him. Hence developed that passionate desire for a direct revelation from God which is an important element in the teachings of Philo as well as in the Neoplatonic doctrines. Even the later Stoics feel the inadequacy of man's will alone and long for divine aid, while the mystic and redemptive religions from the East, among them Christianity, which spread rapidly over the Mediterranean area during the first three centuries of our era, promised in varied forms that aid to secure the soul's salvation.

IV. EASTERN MYSTERIES. EARLY CHRISTIANITY

WE HAVE thus far been concerned with the views of immortality that, native to the Greeks, were gradually spread over the Greco-Roman world before the middle of the third century of our era. But during the later centuries of the long period that we have hastily reviewed, other religions from Asia Minor, Syria, and Egypt made their western conquests. The most notable among these were the cults of the Great Mother of the Gods, of Isis and Osiris, of Mithras, and of Christianity itself. The last we shall leave for the moment. As for the rest, they all in one form or another developed under Hellenic influences into religious mysteries or gave mystic meanings to their original rites, so far as they had not such already, so that they made a powerful appeal to men seeking assurance of protection in this life and of happiness in the world to come.

It is impossible and unnecessary here in our limited space to attempt to describe the mystic rituals of these religions; we need only say that most, if not all, through varied purifications, secret initiations, magic devices, symbolic rites and "divine" revelations gave their initiates assurance of a union with God, ecstatic and brief now, but destined to be permanent hereafter; their devotees were inspired with a hope of security in this world and the next, thereby finding satisfaction for their longing for an unbroken and a perfected existence. These mysteries made wide appeal ultimately to every class in society, beginning perhaps with the poorer and more ignorant, but, as they spread, drawing within their sacred brotherhoods many of the most influential and powerful classes. The ancient mysteries of Greece, as well as those of semi-oriental origin, gained adherents from Rome itself. Of the Greek mysteries those celebrated at Eleusis in Attica were the oldest and most popular. In the later days of republican Rome many prominent men, including Sulla, Antony, Cicero, and Atticus were initiated, drawn partly perhaps by fashion but probably not moved by such a motive alone.[34] Beginning with Augustus, who was initiated in 21 B.C., the mysteries won the following members of the imperial families to their sacred company: Hadrian in A.D. 125, Lucius Verus in 167, Marcus Aurelius and Commodus in 176, Septimus Severus before he became emperor; while Hadrian's wife was honored as a "New Demeter" (Νεὰ Δημήτηρ), as was the elder Faustina, consort of Antoninus Pius. In the fourth century, during the final acute struggle between Paganism and Christianity, many of the Roman nobility eagerly sought initiation into the Eleusinian rites as well as into other pagan mysteries. In fact the popularity of Eleusis lasted until the shrine was destroyed by Alaric and his Goths in A.D. 396. The last records in the entire Roman world of the mystic rites of the Great Mother of the Gods belong to the year A.D. 390. They are found in two inscriptions discovered in the sixteenth century near the present sacristy of St. Peter's. Here was a prominent shrine of the Great Goddess where her purifying and regenerating ritual had been carried on for more than three centuries, until at last, after the first St. Peter's had stood beside the pagan shrine for nearly seventy years, the Great Mother had to yield to the Christ.[35]

The influence of these pagan mysteries has often been exaggerated. They did not by any means completely expel the older gods and the ancient religious practices: the latter continued and indeed in many instances were taken over into Christianity; and some of the pagan divinities were absorbed or metamorphosed into Christian saints. Nevertheless it is true that before the beginning of our era the older forms of religious expression and the ancient religions themselves in a considerable degree had failed. They no longer satisfied man's hopes or provided him with grateful outlets for his religious feeling. Proof of this condition is found also in the large resort of all classes to philosophy, both Epicurean and Stoic, especially to the latter, which fortified the individual against the disappointments and disasters of this life, even if it gave him no hope of recompense beyond; likewise in the devotion of the cultured to the mystic philosophies, Neopythagoreanism and later Neoplatonism, of which the second proved by far the more appealing and satisfying. Stoic philosophy for the sterner wills, the mystic philosophies for the more emotional spirits, and the religious mysteries, Greek, Egyptian, and Anatolian, for many,

[56]

simple and learned alike — these, until Christianity became powerful, were the most vital religious forces in the period between the third century before our era and the third century after Christ.

Further causes for this condition of things are not far to seek. The period was one during which profound political and economic changes took place that transformed the older order and shook the confidence of men's minds. As early as the latter half of the fourth century before Christ, the power of Macedon had destroyed the Greek city-state and checked the freedom that the individual had earlier enjoyed in the Hellenic democracies; and, whatever the reasons may have been, the creative impulse gradually died down in the Greek mind. In the West the storm and stress, both within and without, through which the power of Rome was created, absorbed and satisfied Roman ambitions until near the end of the Republic, when party leaders grew into dictators and the Roman state became the prize for the strongest. Then followed the Empire. For all the wise moderation of its founder, Augustus, before the end of his long reign men had felt the bridle imposed by the imperial government: presently the tyrant appeared in Caligula, to whom Nero and Domitian furnished a proper climax. The terror of the imperial power was first experienced most keenly by Rome and the nearer parts of Italy, but the horrors of the civil strife in the year A.D. 69, through which Nero's successor was determined, affected the whole empire. Cut off from free political activities and weighed down by fears, thoughtful men were turned in upon themselves and forced to find consolation in philosophy or religion. Cicero and Cato of Utica give us notable illustrations from the close of the Republic, while the first century of our era furnishes striking examples, especially among the Stoics. Then the intellectual and noble sought spiritual direction from men like Seneca and Cornutus; in that servile age only a few like Thrasea Paetus and Helvidius Priscus displayed true courage; and the common people resorted to masters like Epictetus for help and guidance.

Fortifying as Stoic philosophy proved for many in every social class of the Greco-Roman world of this time, others of different temper, finding no deep satisfaction in rationalism or in the ancient religious practices of the state, turned to mystic philosophies and to the religious mysteries to which we have just referred. For these philosophies and mysteries through emotional experience and revelation gave promise of that security here and of that salvation hereafter which men desired.

It is important to observe further that during the period of which we are now speaking there had grown up a sense of moral guilt, of an estrangement from the divine through sin that required purification, if man was to obtain freedom from the bondage of wickedness. Moreover, the old idea of man's self-sufficiency had failed: both rationalism and mysticism agreed that man's reason and will could not unaided liberate him from his moral bondage, but that an act of divine grace was required to secure his release; only by divine favor could he obtain that union with God which would give him a sense of security in this world and a promise of entrance into that unbroken and perfected life of which he dreamed. A compensating immortality was the hope of the larger number of those who thought or felt deeply on such subjects. Hence the popularity of Neopythagoreanism and Neoplatonism among the philosophic, and of the mysteries of the Eleusinian divinities, of Bacchus, of Isis and Osiris, Mithras, and the Great Mother of the Gods in the early centuries of our era. The philosophies based their hopes for immortality on Orphic and Platonic beliefs; the religious mysteries relied on revelation and sacraments: all had in varying degrees ethical requirements.

Such in brief were the religious thoughts and sentiments of the Gentile world into which Christianity entered, and such were the chief opponents with which Christianity had to come to an agreement, or destroy, or be itself destroyed.

Now Christianity was the debtor to both Jew and Gentile. In the *Old Testament* we find that the concept of a future retributive life was never a very significant element in Hebrew thought: the abode of the dead was a place much like the Homeric Hades, a region where the shades of former men had at most a negative existence, for they were cut off from the upper world and from Jahweh alike. Job cries in his despair: " For there is hope of a tree, if it be cut down, that it will sprout again, and that the tender branch thereof will not cease. Though the root thereof wax old in the earth, and the stock thereof die in the ground; yet through the scent of water it will bud, and put forth boughs like a plant. But man dieth, and wasteth away: yea, man giveth up the ghost, and where is he? As the waters fail from the sea, and the river decayeth and drieth up; so man lieth down and riseth not: till the heavens be no more, they shall not awake, nor be roused out of their sleep." [36] And again he asks without hope: "If a man die, shall he live again?" [37] There is no assurance that in Sheol the undeserved misfortunes of the righteous will be compensated by due rewards; the most for which man can hope is that his shade may be aware of what is done in the world of the living. The resurrection which is promised by the Vulgate and modern versions in the nineteenth chapter is not warranted in the original.[38]

In the post-exilic period the Jews had hoped for a material kingdom of God on earth, a golden age which the whole nation should enjoy; but gradually this expectation of a national, and, so to speak, of a political kingdom was transformed into a hope for a spiritual kingdom to be established at some future time either on a transformed earth or in a supermundane heaven; into this nobler kingdom only the righteous, both the dead and those then living, were to be admitted through God's mercy; but the wicked were doomed to eternal punishment or to utter annihilation.[39]

Under Persian and Greek influence this concept of a retributive age to come in which the individual would receive his recompense of joy or punishment gradually grew; yet the Jews never reached the position where the individual's future was separated from that of the whole body of the people. In the book of *Daniel*, however, the resurrection is set forth in a form that is reminiscent of earlier Jewish thought; the Wisdom of Solomon on the other hand shows the effect of Greek influence, giving, as it does, a view of immortality largely in accord with Platonic ideas; for this book represents the views of those Jews who at Alexandria and in other Hellenic centers had felt the power of their environment. Still many Jews clung to the older views and rejected the notion of the resurrection entirely.[40]

In the time of Jesus, as later, there was current a great variety of ideas among the Jews as to the nature of a life hereafter, as well as doubts as to the existence of such a life; but all who believed in the resurrection regarded the future life as retributive; and this fact is the one that is of prime religious importance in our present consideration.[41]

Jesus apparently took the resurrection of the righteous at least for granted, and, so far as our documents go, he did not trouble himself to advance any arguments to prove the existence of a life beyond this. Such an attitude was natural enough, for the majority of his hearers probably believed in some kind of a future existence. Nor do we find in his teaching any philosophic discussion of the nature of the soul and its relation to the body. Jesus was a religious teacher of simple men, and had no occasion to be philosopher or theologian. But using ideas familiar to his followers through inheritance, he gave them richer content and often new meaning. To take a single illustration on a cardinal point, he transformed the Jewish concepts of the kingdom of God and of the righteous man's share therein, by his teaching that the divine kingdom is here on earth and will continue in heaven; or, to speak more accurately, that the kingdom is eternal. It is true that Jesus inevitably spoke of this kingdom in terms of time and space, and that he held that man's present experience of it would be consummated in the future. The significant thing is that Jesus felt the kingdom of God to be a present reality rather than something to the enjoyment of which man might attain in the future. The righteous, who for him included all who desire to do the will of God, even those who repent at the eleventh hour, because they are righteous, enjoy that kingdom now, provided that they recognize their relation to God to be that of loving sons to a loving father and therefore love their fellow men: love of God and love of man were to him the sources of genuine righteousness.

It is unnecessary at this point to go further into the teachings of Jesus on the future life in general; and still less need we delay here to discuss his teachings as to his later coming and the day of judgment, important as these matters have generally been in the minds of his followers. On some of these points, however, it will be necessary to touch in the later discussion.

Naturally the belief in their Lord's resurrection was for his followers sufficient warrant and proof that they too would rise into a new life after physical death; and the belief that Christ rose from the dead has been the basis of

Christian hope ever since. The familiar passage in Paul's *First Epistle to the Corinthians* has become the final statement of the Christian faith on this point; and the apostle's figurative use of the same argument in writing to the Christians in Thessalonica shows how fundamental and familiar the doctrine early became.

When we examine the Pauline writings more closely, we find that we are dealing with a set of ideas inherited from earlier Judaism, probably influenced by Hellenistic thought, and profoundly modified by the writer's own experience. From Jewish thought he had inherited the belief that man is made up of flesh ($\sigma\acute{\alpha}\rho\xi$) and spirit ($\pi\nu\epsilon\hat{\upsilon}\mu\alpha$) both of which are necessary to constitute his personality. Although in his own experience he had known well the conflict between these two elements, he probably did not think of the flesh as inherently wicked, as the Orphics and Platonists believed, but rather as the seat or ally of sin which makes the members of the body war against the mind ($\nu o\hat{\upsilon}s$).[42] And yet we may suspect that Paul, who for all his clear thinking was neither metaphysician, nor theologian, nor psychologist, had hardly escaped completely the influence of Greek thought which cannot have been unknown at Tarsus and Jerusalem, and which may well have penetrated into the circle about Gamaliel. Whatever were the sources of Paul's views on the nature of man it is undeniable that he ordinarily draws an ethical contrast between the flesh and the spirit: to be carnally minded is death, to be spiritually minded is life and peace. Now it is evident that this view in its practical bearings is closely parallel to the Greek belief in the dualism of man, which in one form or another was common to most Hellenistic philosophies. Therefore an alliance was easily made between Pauline views and those of the Greco-Roman world, and on this association much of the history of Christian thought depends.

The Pharisees, of whom Paul was one, held a firm belief in the resurrection of the body; on which point Paul's views were confirmed by his belief that Jesus had risen from the grave and had appeared in the flesh to men who had recognized him by his familiar features. But for the identical body Paul substituted a spiritual or heavenly one which the soul should inhabit hereafter. His concept of the soul as well as of the body was doubtless material: both the resurrected body and the soul were thought by him to be made of tenuous matter, as was natural for one of his training and antecedents to believe. Yet any doctrine of the resurrection of any kind of body was difficult for most Gentiles, since the Platonic view that the soul was immaterial was widely held among those Greeks who had not embraced Stoic or Epicurean materialism. Evidently the Corinthian converts had had some difficulties in believing that the body could rise from the tomb to clothe the soul, and moreover they probably had been accustomed to think of the soul as an entity by itself. Paul's answer to them is the famous fifteenth chapter of his first letter to their church. In this he argues that man's personality is not spiritual alone, or solely corporeal, but is both, which are necessary to his being: consequently man's personality must continue to be essentially the same in the world beyond; therefore there must be a resurrection of the body. Yet common sense and countless analogies from nature prove to him that it would not be the same as the terrestrial one, subject to corruption, but a celestial body incorruptible. For this concept, as has been said above, Paul found full warrant in the resurrection of Christ and his appearance in glory. He does not build up an elaborate eschatology, but centers all his argument on the risen Christ.

Yet Paul's views did not determine wholly the main lines of Christian thought. The *Epistle to the Hebrews* seems to show divergence at most points from his views, especially perhaps in the matter of resurrection of the body, on which subject the writer of this letter has absolutely nothing to say; nor does he discuss a material heaven hereafter; but he holds that those who have been redeemed by the blood of Christ are to enjoy an eternal Sabbath in the celestial city.[43]

The *Fourth Gospel* and the Johannine epistles represent a further stage in the development of Christian thought. The prologue to the Gospel is the earliest attempt to square the concepts of the new religion with secular philosophy and thus to make the new ideas intelligible to the Hellenistic world: Christ is presented as eternal and divine, the Logos of philosophic speech, who by His incarnation revealed God to man. Through belief in Jesus as the incarnate Word of God men may obtain that knowledge of the truth that will make them free; through belief in Christ they experience a new birth in the spirit whereby they enter now into eternal life. There is no picture of the future life in the Johannine writings from which we can determine whether the writer or writers held to the resurrection of the body or otherwise: the whole emphasis is on the present experience of eternal life won by faith in Christ and testified to by love for God and man.

The *Revelation* of John, a work which by its content and nature belongs to a long series of Jewish visions, has had a great influence on Christian eschatological ideas, even to the present day. According to the unknown writer, after the beast and the false prophet have been slain, the hosts of the kings of the earth destroyed, and Satan bound for a thousand years, then the martyrs and the faithful saints shall rise and reign with Christ on earth for a millennium; when this era is finished, Satan shall be loosed from his bonds, and then shall follow the war of Gog and Magog who shall in turn be destroyed by fire from heaven; the Devil shall be cast into the lake of fire and brimstone where the beast and the false prophet are, to be tortured forever and ever. After this shall come the general resurrection and the last judgment which shall allot to the righteous a never ending life in the New Jerusalem, the material splendor of which surpasses earthly experience, while the wicked are to suffer a second death, having their part in the lake that burneth with fire and brimstone.

The ideas of this book come from Jewish tradition, but they were eventually accepted by the majority of Christians, learned and simple alike, so that a millennial reign of Christ on earth, the corporeal resurrection, and the materialistic eschatology consonant with it have been orthodox beliefs in no small proportion of churches.

Thus at about the beginning of the second Christian century we may picture the infant church as entertaining certain conflicting ideas as to the soul's future state. These ideas were derived from Judaism past and contemporaneous, from Greek philosophic concepts, and from efforts to reconcile the two. There was, it is true, general agreement as to the redemptive mission of Christ, and all saw in his resurrection the warrant for the resurrection of the faithful. But whether the righteous alone were to be raised from the dead to everlasting joy, or whether all were to rise, the faithful and the wicked alike, each to his appropriate award, were matters for dispute; many held to the literal resurrection of the physical body, others cherished a belief in the revival of a spiritualized body; Greek dualistic concepts of the flesh as material and evil and of the soul as spiritual and appetitive of God, prevented many from accepting any doctrine of the post-mundane existence of a body; while large numbers found satisfaction in hopes of a kingdom of God on earth or in a materialistic heavenly city. Few men in any age are either philosophers or theologians: the majority think only of the visible man as the real man and therefore imagine him as enjoying a future existence, if such there be, in very much his present corporeal form.

But early a majority of the Christians were Greeks or people more or less Hellenized in thought, so that Greek ideas were bound to assert themselves, especially the Platonic concept of the soul as an indestructible entity, a part of the substance of God. Against such a view the Jewish interpretation of the mission, suffering, and death of Jesus was distinctly opposed, for if the soul was to be regarded as naturally immortal, of the very substance of

God, and as naturally inclined toward the Good, the conception of the passion and death of Christ as a redemptive sacrifice could hardly be regarded as indispensable; yet it might be cherished without inconsistency as making possible for every striving soul the happiness that in Plato's plan was open to only a few philosophic spirits. The evidence in the early Church writers is clear that much confusion of thought prevailed until Augustine by his genius clarified Christian doctrine through the adoption of a modified form of Neoplatonism. His system in no slight degree determined the course of thinking within the church on the question of immortality down to the latter part of the nineteenth century.

A few illustrations of the difference in views among the early Christian writers will be illuminating. We shall begin with the question whether all are to be raised from the dead or only the righteous. The author of the *First Epistle of Clement* (*c.* A.D. 75–100) apparently had no expectation that the wicked would be revived to any future life, but only the righteous, for whose resurrection he found warrant not only in the resurrection of Jesus Christ, but also in the course of Nature, in the phoenix rising from his own ashes, and in the ancient scriptures. But Ignatius, writing to the Christians of Smyrna (*c.* A.D. 100), seems to believe that the wicked and the righteous alike shall be judged, and judgment presupposes reward or punishment; yet he does not expressly include the wicked in the resurrection. The *Didache* (second century) for its part limits the resurrection of the dead to the saints; and the *Epistle of Barnabas* (*c.* A.D. 130) is not quite clear. It seems to imply that the wicked perish, while the righteous, sanctified by the sprinkled blood of the Lord, are to be raised in triumph over death. Justin (*c.* A.D. 150) looks forward on the contrary to the resurrection of both the just and the unjust, who are to receive again their own bodies; he also holds that sensation will continue in the next world as in this life. Yet in his dialogue with Trypo he maintains against Plato that the soul is not immortal by nature and that only those who appear worthy in God's sight are never to die; the wicked are to continue to exist and to suffer punishment as long as God wills. Athenagoras on the other hand (*c.* A.D. 175–200) assumes that the soul is immortal and argues vigorously in favor of the resurrection of the body, not of the same body that man had on earth, but of a body suited to its new environment.[44]

In general we may say that the Greek Apologists argued against a belief in the natural immortality of the soul, but some felt the force of the Greek view that natural immortality and divinity were equivalent terms. Theophilus, however, after stating his position that God has made man capable only of immortality or death saves the divine justice and grace by arguing that if man regard the teaching of God and incline toward immortality he will receive from God the reward of immortal life and himself become God. Thus he secures man's free will and saves the divine.[45]

How potent the influence of Platonic philosophy was is shown by the pains at which Tertullian is to refute the philosophic doctrine in his treatise "On the Soul." This Latin Father of the Church held that the soul is formed by the breath of God, in the manner described in the book of *Genesis*, not out of gross matter; therefore the soul has a beginning, coming into existence with the body at the moment of conception; yet it is corporeal in very much the Stoic sense; it is distinguished from the "spirit," for the latter is soul in action or the activity of the soul and it is not identical with the mind (*animus*, *νοῦς*). By nature the soul is immortal; it is free to determine its own action, and it has a bodily form. Its purity is marred from its beginning by the evil spirit which regards it with envy; hence it is unclean until divine grace has given it spiritual regeneration. At death souls go to Hades within the earth where they await resurrection; but before that great event each soul begins to receive its due reward, the wicked its punishment, the righteous its joy; but the souls of the martyrs enter at once into Paradise, which according to the *Revelation* of John is not identical with Heaven, but is " under the altar." Tertullian's treatise " On the Resurrection of the Flesh " is an attack on the Gnostics who held that the body is by nature evil, being created by a demiurge hostile to the true God. Man's soul, however, they believed tended toward righteousness and immortality. Against such Platonic dualism the Latin Father vigorously argues, apparently holding that both body and soul are essential to human personality: he maintains that the body is created by God and draws arguments from Hebrew and Christian scriptures, from Nature, and from the person of Christ, to establish his contention that the identical substance of the body will rise at the judgment and that the righteous will enter Heaven not as disembodied souls but as entire human beings having both bodies and souls; and in the same way the wicked will go to the place of their eternal punishment.[46]

But the closing paragraphs of Tertullian's argument show that the dualistic view which was inherent in all Greek thought dependent on Plato, as well as the doctrine of natural immortality of the soul, would not down in spite of the efforts of the Fathers, who, with good reason, saw in the latter claim a denial that any redemptive grace was necessary for man.

The Greek Apologists assumed that virtue and knowledge would secure mortal men resurrection into an immortal life, but they did not show how this was to be accomplished: in the resurrection of Christ they found simply assurance of their faith that man also would rise; they interpreted the passion of Christ in accord with Jewish ideas of sacrifice, which were not wholly foreign to the Gentile world. But nevertheless the method by which knowledge and virtue were to change the mortal into the immortal was left unexplained.

Irenaeus, however, like Ignatius at an earlier time and his own disciple, Hippolytus, went into the matter more deeply, recognizing that the bestowal of immortality deified man's nature. He explained the process by pointing out that Christ is the incarnate God, the possessor of immortality, who through genuine union with mortal nature deified it by adoption. Thus man, being created by God, is capable of incorruption and immortality; yet as a created being he is not naturally immortal but is granted immortality through God's union with mortal flesh; therefore life becomes a gift of God's grace. Thus Christ was recognized as the great central fact in human history.[47]

In his eschatology, however, Irenaeus is as unable as others to break away from the expectation of a material kingdom of Christ on earth. The inconsistency of this view with his concept of the redemptive Christ as God incarnate in mortal flesh is glaring to us today, but it is easily explicable on historical grounds. No detailed account of his view need here be given, for he does not essentially differ on this point from other writers of the second and third centuries.[48]

V. GNOSTICS. CLEMENT ORIGEN

I T IS important to observe that a gulf separates the Greek Apologists from men like
Irenaeus, and still more from Hippolytus.
For the former group, morality, right conduct,
based on a correct theory of the world was
sufficient to insure mortals an immortal life, as
we have said above; but the latter were rather
akin to the more mystic Greek philosophers
and the Greek mysteries in holding that mortal
man in acquiring immortality becomes divine,
a God indeed, as Hippolytus expressly says.[49]
In this way again Christian faith was brought
into accord with Greek thought, and the spread
of Christian ideas among the philosophically
minded was made the easier throughout the
Greek world.

But in this Hellenic world there had existed
for centuries a belief that it was by revelation
alone that supreme knowledge was attainable
— such knowledge as conferred perfection on
its possessor. This belief was implicit in Or-

phism, Pythagoreanism, and may be detected at many points in Plato's thought — for example, in his vision of the Good ($αὐτὸ τὸ καλόν$) which his statesmen would enjoy; for although this vision was to be won in part by long years of severe discipline, it was also in part a revelation which would suddenly come to the devout.[50] In the various mysteries, the initiated through emotional experience attained, as they believed, a secret knowledge ($γνῶσις$) which could not be won by the *profani*. As we have already seen, the later secular thinkers who were influenced by Plato, philosophers like Philo and Plotinus, all relied on direct revelation for the attainment of the highest knowledge. This tendency, which thus long antedated Christianity, had naturally appeared early among Christian thinkers, who, if they desired, could bring the *Old Testament* to support their doctrine as well as certain words of the Apostle Paul, for he had claimed that his knowledge and the Gospel that he preached had come to him directly " by the revelation of Jesus Christ." [51] The Gnostics, a name given to groups of men who displayed the greatest diversity of beliefs and morals, were found in many areas where Christianity

was established. Although they were ultimately denounced as heretical, they did a certain valuable and permanent service to Christianity in that they vigorously attempted to
give a philosophic interpretation of it as the
supreme religion which replaced paganism and
Judaism. They also regarded the Redeemer
as the one who completed the development of
humanity and consummated the history of the
universe. Such a philosophy of history was in
general in accord with the view of Christians
everywhere, but the Gnostics were more thoroughgoing than most of their fellows: they rejected the *Old Testament* since the new revelation in Christ had supplanted it; and they
exalted esoteric knowledge ($\gamma\nu\tilde{\omega}\sigma\iota\varsigma$) above
faith ($\pi\iota\sigma\tau\iota\varsigma$) as the fundamental element in
their religion. Following the universal system
of allegorical interpretation, they found in the
Apostolic writings, which at their face value
gave the rule of faith for the masses, an inner
and deeper meaning which was to be gained
only by those who could detect their secret
messages. Thus the Gnostics recognized two
grades of Christians: the ordinary mass who
lacked insight, and who therefore must live by
faith alone without deep knowledge of things

divine; and the few who, blessed with the power to see below the surface, were able to attain to supreme knowledge. These favored ones thus corresponded to Plato's statesmen in his ideal state.

The Gnostics generally held to a pretty complete dualism which put God and matter at diameter with each other: at one pole was matter, evil by nature; at the other was the perfectly transcendent Being above all thought. Into the details of the ways in which, through many emanations, they bridged the gap between God and the World, we need not now go, but we may remark that the Gnostic views were simply somewhat more extravagant devices for doing that which Philo and the later Platonists managed with comparative restraint.

Naturally the Gnostics took the Platonic view that man is made up of a corruptible body and a divine spirit; yet they held that not all men were capable of salvation. Some of more spiritual nature were assured of a life of bliss hereafter; but the more material among mankind were doomed to perish. The followers of Valentinus, the famous Gnostic leader who was active at Rome (*c.* 140–*c.* 165), went further and conceived, still in Platonic fashion, of three classes of men: the material, who would be destroyed; the animal, who might by correct choice find repose in the " intermediate habitation "; but the spiritual, being incapable of corruption, would attain perfection and be given " as brides to the angels of the Saviour." [52] The resurrection of the physical body of Christ they were unable to accept; but Paul had already shown them the way out of this difficulty: the resurrection was to be understood in a spiritual sense. They claimed that the real resurrection is of the spirit, not of the flesh; and indeed that the genuine Gnostic who has gained insight into divine mysteries through possession of true knowledge ($\gamma\nu\hat{\omega}\sigma\iota\varsigma$) has already risen into the spiritual state, so that the resurrection for him is already passed; for the resurrection of the dead is nothing but a recognition of the truth which they declare.[53]

The Gnostic movement in its manifold phases thus represents attempts to combine Christianity with Greek and certain oriental elements in ways that diverged from the normal course of orthodox thought in degrees varying from simple docetism to the most extravagant and fantastic imaginings; its most important effect was to stimulate the more orthodox to form a catholic doctrine which could win the adherence of the great majority of believers and so protect the church by a bulwark of reasonable dogma, widely acceptable to intelligent men. Yet the influence of the Gnostics may be detected in many details of the doctrines that were finally accepted.[54]

Nowhere did Jewish, Greek, and Christian ideas come into closer and more intensive contact than in Alexandria, which for three centuries before our era had been the chief intellectual center of the Mediterranean world. There science, letters, criticism, and speculative thought flourished; it was one of the chief Gnostic centers under the leadership of Basileides, who was active during the reign of Hadrian (117–138). At the close of the second century of our era a Christian catechetical school became important there, which was heir not only to secular thought and pagan mysticism, but to the Christian Gnostics and Apologists. In this school both Greek philosophy and the Holy Scriptures were studied under two of the greatest minds in the history of the Church: Clement, who was first pupil, then teacher, and finally for about three years head of the school (200–202/3), and Origen, director

[83]

of the school from 203 to 231. To them we must now turn.

As we have intimated above, thus far no satisfactory Christian theology had been systematically developed; but the time had now arrived when such a system was needed, as has just been said, to win over intellectual disciples whose rational habit of mind could not be satisfied by a rule of faith based on the Scriptures alone. To this task Clement and Origen turned. The former was intimately acquainted with Greek philosophy and letters, as well as with the Scriptures and the interpretations thereof by both orthodox and Gnostic teachers. His learning and eloquence drew Pagans and Christians alike to hear him. He was the first to attempt to explain Christianity with all the aid that Greek learning and heretical speculation had to give: he showed that reasoning men had a right to an exposition that could satisfy their intelligence; moreover, he believed that such a rational explanation was at no point at variance with the rule of faith. He claimed for himself the title of the true Gnostic, for in his *Miscellanies* (Στρωματεῖς), a work intended to establish Christianity as the true philosophy, after combating Gnostic errors, he gives much space to a presentation of the position and character of the true Gnostic.[55] He agreed with his Gnostic predecessors in holding that there must be two grades of Christians: the ordinary Christian will be forced to direct his life according to faith, and such is the lower Christian life; but one who is capable of a profounder insight may through study and discipline attain to supreme knowledge and to a life higher morally and intellectually than that of the ordinary believer. According to him, the lower grade of Christian life is marked by faith, fear, and hope; the higher by love, righteousness, and knowledge.[56] Thus Clement, in his turn, put himself in accord with the whole range of philosophic thought from the time of Plato and Aristotle to his own day, for his two lives are essentially the active and the contemplative lives that for more than five centuries had been distinguished by philosophers; only now in both secular philosophy and religion alike the higher life was conceived to be one which brought to him who enjoyed it a divine revelation. Clement held that this revelation gave its recipient direct communion with the eternal ideas of which Christ, the Logos, is the sum; but since Christ is the Son of God, coequal with

Him, the true Gnostic apprehends God in His Son — indeed, the Lord is Himself the true Light and the true Knowledge; and this knowledge comprehends all. The true Gnostic is also holy and righteous, given to prayer and to spiritual exercise.

Important as Clement is in the history of the development of Christian thought and dogma, it was his pupil and successor, Origen, who established Christian theology as a philosophic system; in spite of the fact that the Church fairly promptly rejected much of his system in detail, his influence was great and permanent. We are not called on to trace here his theological system even in outline; let it suffice to say that he carried on the work of Clement to its logical conclusion; yet at many points he modified his teacher's doctrines. Although he was faithful in holding fast to the *Old* and *New Testaments* as containing the sum of Christian truth and to the traditional teaching of the growing Church, he did not hesitate to embark freely on philosophic speculation; tradition says that he had listened to the teaching of Ammonius Saccas, the founder of the Neoplatonic School, and indeed his work shows many signs of the influence of Gnosticism and

Neoplatonism. It is clear that his thought was in agreement with the secular speculation of his time.

Origen's human psychology was doubtless derived in large measure from his teacher, Clement, whose views, like those of the Gnostics, as we have already said, go back ultimately to Plato and Aristotle. He held that man, in common with all other living creatures, possesses a lower animal soul which comes into existence at the moment of conception, and which gives man physical life; and a higher, a spiritual soul, which is bestowed on man from above. This latter soul is a fallen spirit, which in falling has become a human soul; but it may develop into a spirit once more and thus regain its spiritual endowments. God in the beginning had granted freedom to men who fell by evil choice, so that all are born into a sinful condition. Man's duty is to overcome his inherent sin by his own will aided by God's grace, to give the mastery over himself to the divine soul within him, that he may become like God and thereby secure eternal happiness. Strictly speaking, Origen's system does not require a redeemer, but nevertheless he does bring into his scheme of salvation the historic revelation of the Logos and the death of Christ, which he regarded as the first blow in the struggle against the devil.[57]

Origen agreed with Clement and the followers of Basileides in holding that there are three levels of the Christian life, or three stages of Christian progress. He thought that in the first the Logos, incarnate in the historic Christ, serves as a physician to cure men of their errors and sins, and that those who will, by faith and a belief in the redemption given by the death of the historic Christ, may attain to freedom from sin and to fellowship with God. In the second stage the enlightened and righteous soul, no longer needing the Redeemer to heal from sin, may rise above the phenomenal world to the "invisible things of God" (τὰ ἀόρατα τοῦ θεοῦ . . . τουτ᾽ ἔστι τὰ νοητά). This stage, then, is attained by the purified soul through the exercise of intelligence, so that it comprehends the whole creation. But from this the soul may soar to still greater heights and attain to "the eternal power of God, in short, to his divinity" (ἀναβαίνουσι ἐπὶ τὴν ἀΐδιον δύναμιν τοῦ θεοῦ καὶ ἀπαξαπλῶς τὴν θεότητα αὐτοῦ). These words must mean that in the highest phase the soul enjoys that direct knowledge of God, wins that Beatific Vision, which is to be the everlasting joy of the Saints, the possession and reward of the true Gnostic.[58]

In contrast to the great majority of his time both within and without the Church, Origen would not believe in a future state of sensuous joys or sufferings; nor did he hold that the resurrection of the dead must await the second coming of Christ. He rather thought that at physical death the pure and righteous souls would enter directly into Paradise, while the wicked would begin to suffer their punishment at once. Both would be provided with bodies; yet these would not be the same as those which they possessed on earth, but spiritual bodies fitted to their new plane of existence. The bodies of the righteous would be more beautiful than any known on earth, free from all material attributes, with no superfluous organs, but bright and shining like the angels and the stars; the wicked, however, would receive bodies opaque and black, corresponding to the depths of ignorance and error in which they had lived on earth. The righteous would mount upward, and when their perfection should be fully accomplished, they would become pure intelligence as they were in the beginning before they fell from Heaven into sin; the wicked would indeed suffer their fiery punishment, but this, like the whole course of man's existence, would be remedial: the fire would not be a physical fire to consume the flesh, but a figurative one — the pangs and sufferings of conscience for past sins. Ultimately all would be purified and restored through Christ, the Word.[59] Yet both Clement and Origen taught that man would be free in the next life as in this, so that his soul might fall even from the greatest heights to the lowest depths, as it could rise from the deepest moral abyss to supreme purity and blessedness. The future life, then, in Origen's view is to be one of cleansing for all who do not resist the purpose of God, but who strive to satisfy man's love of righteousness which he has implanted in them.[60]

Origen's doctrine of man's free will is evidently in conflict with his view of man's longing for righteousness and with his belief in God's grace. In fact he found it hard to believe that any man could be condemned to punishment without end; and he was not able to think that evil spirits were beyond the possibility of salvation in the infinite time that belongs to God. In any case he cherished hopes for even the vilest of human sinners. His humane sentiments and his belief in God's goodness thus triumphed over strict logic. We might say, in fact, in terms that are somewhat misleading from their modern connotations, that he cherished a belief in the constant possibility of moral and spiritual evolution or devolution *in saecula saeculorum* according to man's will, but at the same time he declined to regard any soul as beyond ultimate salvation.

The real bases of his views on the ultimate salvability of all are to be found in Plato; in the *Gorgias* especially, proof is offered that goodness and justice are ultimately identical; that suffering is remedial to restore man from the disease of evil to the health of uprightness; and that evil is created by man in opposition to God, and being thus made is a negation which must ultimately cease to be, so that in the end perfect righteousness shall have undisputed sway. These Platonic views Origen supported with sundry texts from both the *Old* and the *New Testament*. There can, in truth, be no question that he hoped for the final restitution of all souls, and the charges of universalism brought against him in ancient and modern times have not been without foundation.[61]

The Alexandrian fathers held not only to moral progress in the future life but also believed in a change in the soul's abode. The scientific theory of antiquity from at least the fourth century B.C. was that the heavens consisted of seven concentric spheres corresponding to the seven planets; and that beyond the seventh heaven was the eighth, the fixed sphere ($\dot{a}\pi\lambda\alpha\nu\dot{\eta}s$ $\sigma\phi\alpha\hat{\imath}\rho\alpha$) where dwells the eternal One. The Gnostics, Pagan and Christian, held a theory that the soul would ascend through the several heavens, the degree of its ascent being determined by its perfection.[62] To this theory Clement subscribed. Only the true Gnostic could pass on to the uppermost sphere where he would dwell eternally with Christ, enjoying the direct vision of God to which the pure in heart alone may attain.[63] On these Gnostic views of his teacher Origen entertained some doubts, for he could not find them adequately established in the sacred writings; yet his own ideas were simply more vague than those of Clement, for he allowed a multiplicity of heavens, a series of aeons reaching to the Consummation.[64] This was attainable only by the perfect: the pure in heart alone could enjoy the Beatific Vision; for the imperfect, even though finally freed from chastisement, the eternal punishment of deprivation remained: they were to find each his place in the ascending scale of joy, but they were not to see God face to face.[65] Thus absolute universalism is not the logical result of the teachings of either Clement or Origen, for, according to them, the great majority of mankind, even after the purging of remorse and shame had ceased, must still suffer everlasting punishment for their sins in exclusion from the Vision of God, which deprivation is the *poena damni*. Sinful men, though cured of their sins, could never attain the supreme place.

The limitations of our subject forbid us to enlarge here on Origen's theology, which actually dominated parts of the Eastern Church for some centuries, in spite of bitter censures, and had a deep influence on the West, condemned though it was by the patriarch Theophilus and the synod of Alexandria (399/400). Pope Anastasius at Rome (398–402) reproved Rufinus for translating the *De Principiis* and joined in the condemnation of Origen's doctrines, as Jerome was eager to have him do.

In A.D. 496 Pope Gelasius declared Origen a schematic, and in the East Origen and his followers were condemned under Justinian. All this, however, belongs to the historian of the church. We need only observe now that Origen for the first time disposed of the vagaries of Gnosticism by reconciling the Christian rule of faith with Greek philosophy. This, however, he did not for the mass but for the intellectuals who were capable of thinking theologically, that is, philosophically. Further accommodation had to be made before Greek philosophy could be thoroughly recognized within the Church.

VI. GREGORY OF NYSSA.
MACARIUS. PSEUDO–DIONYSIUS

THE PROFOUND influence of Platonic thought on Clement and Origen needs no further illustration here. The power of that philosophy continued to be dominant both East and West in secular and Christian circles. It can be seen, for example, in the works of that opponent of Origen, Methodius, bishop of Olympus in Lycia († 311), who was less successful, however, in his use of Platonic literary forms than in his attempts to grasp the doctrines of the successive Platonic schools.[66] More significant in general are the three mighty Cappadocians, Basil the Great (*c.* 330–379), his brother Gregory of Nyssa (331–394), and Gregory of Nazianzus (*c.* 330–379), all of whom held Origen in high regard. The first and last, however, do not so much concern us now, for, although Basil's theological and ethical views were strongly influenced by Platonic and Cynic thought,[67] and in spite of his valiant attack on the Arians, his work was primarily that of a practical genius whose rules for the religious life are still influential in the Greek Orthodox church; his close friend Gregory of Nazianzus, inspired likewise by ancient learning and fired by Christian zeal, eloquently defended the orthodox doctrine of the Trinity, especially in his famous five "Theological Speeches."[68] Gregory of Nyssa, however, is important for our present consideration. Hitherto ecclesiastical writers had not made a sharp distinction between reason and the faith that is inspired by revelation, but had been inclined to regard reason and faith as being in natural accord, holding the former to be of equal value as the latter. But with Gregory of Nyssa philosophy began to serve as the handmaid of faith, for to his thinking the Scriptures alone contain the absolute truth: all reasoning not in accord with faith is therefore erroneous.[69] His treatise "On the Soul and the Resurrection" is of prime significance for our theme. Although this dialogue is modeled on Plato's *Phaedo,* its matter has much in common with Cicero's *Tusculan Disputations;* and the influence of Origen is manifest throughout.

In opposition to Plato, however, Gregory

held that the soul of man has had no eternal
existence, but in each case is created by God;
since it is endowed with thought it is not a
material but a spiritual substance, not identical
with God but, as we may say, a copy of Him.
The divine image in man's soul, however, is
obscured through sin which alienates him from
God; repentance and a new birth are necessary
to restore him to his original condition.

Because the human soul is simple and uncompounded it can survive the destruction of
the body, which is a composite thing. Yet
when the body is dissolved, the soul can ac-
company and watch the particles of which its
former corporeal home was composed until the
resurrection, when it will again clothe itself in
a renewed body — the celestial body of which
St. Paul conceived.[70]

To Gregory's mind punishment after this
life is to be proportionate to sin and always
remedial, that the wicked soul may be purged
of its impurities, and when wholly cleansed
may appear as the very image of Divinity. In
God is the only true life with which the soul
can be satisfied. Thus the resurrection will
be completed in the restoration of the purified
man to his original state (ἀνάστασίς ἐστιν ἡ εἰς

τὸ ἀρχαῖον τῆς φύσεως ἡμῶν ἀποκατάστασις), that is, to the pure condition that it enjoyed at the time of its creation by God.[71]

In this way Gregory of Nyssa shows a firm belief in the overruling providence of God, who chastises only that the human soul may be cleansed of evil and at last in purity return to its maker. Thus far he is in large degree heir unwittingly perhaps to Plato and the Orphics. They, however, seem to have allowed obstinate sinners to suffer everlasting punishment. But Gregory's confidence in the goodness of God led him to believe that ultimately all, even the Evil One himself, will return to union with God: for Gregory as for Origen universal salvation is the final stage.

Although Gregory would prove his doctrines by reasoned arguments whenever possible, he also displays the same mystic tendencies that we found in Clement and Origen: indeed he was the first to attempt to formulate a mystic system for Christianity. This mysticism was based on the doctrine that man's soul is the image of God, for which Gregory found his warrant in faith in Holy Scripture (*Gen.*, I. 36 f.), since reason gave him no support here.[72] He argued that through such resemblance of the human to the Divine we can gain a better understanding of the supernatural character of our souls; and furthermore he believed that even though man may not see the Divine directly face to face, he who with all diligence cleanses his heart of the filth that has defiled it may discern within his own soul the very image of God.[73]

But Gregory did not condemn the faithful Christian to dependence on imagery alone for his knowledge of God: like Philo and the Neoplatonists, he held that in holy ecstasy the soul might, although through a cloud, obtain a vision of the Divine that is beyond all vision: "As the mind of man goes forward and proceeds through ever greater and more perfect advance in understanding of real knowledge, the more it approaches the sight of God, the more it perceives that the divine nature is invisible. For when it has left behind not only all that the senses perceive but also all that the mind seems to grasp, it goes ever on to that which lies farther within, until at last freed from the trouble of thought, it escapes to that which is invisible and incomprehensible, and there sees God. For the true knowledge of the object of our search, the Vision of God, con-

sists in seeing that He cannot be seen, since
that which we seek is above all knowledge, being wholly wrapped as it were in a mist, its own
incomprehensibility. Therefore John the Sub-
lime also, who had himself entered into this
bright mist, says that no man hath seen God
at any time, meaning by this denial that the
knowledge of the divine nature is impossible
not only for man but for every intelligent
creature." [74]

A similar tendency toward mysticism may
be seen more fully developed in the East in
the works of Macarius the Egyptian (c. 300–
390) and of the Pseudo-Dionysius (c. 500).
In contrast with Gregory of Nyssa, and with
most Christian writers of his time, Macarius
emphasized the material nature of the human
soul, which he claims to be corporeal like the
angels and daemons (ἐπεὶ καὶ ἕκαστον κατὰ
τὴν ἰδίαν φύσιν σῶμά ἐστιν, ὁ ἄγγελος, ἡ ψυχή,
ὁ δαίμων).[75] The soul has not an eternal existence but is a creation, intelligent, beautiful,
noble, and marvelous, a fair likeness and image
of God (ἡ ψυχὴ . . . ἔστι κτίσμα τι νοερὸν
καὶ ὡραῖον καὶ μέγα καὶ θαυμαστόν, καὶ καλὸν
ὁμοίωμα καὶ εἰκὼν θεοῦ). In comparison with
the body it is made up of the finest matter

($\pi\nu\epsilon\hat{v}\mu\alpha$), so that it pervades and comprehends the whole body, "the eye with which it sees, the ear with which it hears, the tongue with which it speaks, and every part, being commingled with the whole." God alone is incorporeal, pure spirit. But through love for man God diminished himself, assumed and entered into a body, thus making possible the union of the souls of saints and angels with Himself, and thereby giving them a share in the divine life. In this way God ever takes to Himself faithful and acceptable souls, and becomes with them *one* spirit: the souls that are worthy of Him and find favor in His sight may therefore enter into a new condition, become conscious of immortality, and share in the eternal glory.[76]

Yet Macarius held that the human soul in its own character does not partake either of the divine nature or of the nature of wickedness, but is capable of sharing in either. It is created as an image of God, it is true, but this heavenly image may be driven out through sin, and it can be regained only through the new birth from God and the redemption given by God incarnate. Macarius, however, with good practical sense, constantly emphasized the

need on man's part of right desire and of de-
termination to prove himself worthy of God's
favor and of a share in the Holy Spirit; nevertheless, he did not hold that man's effort alone
could win for him salvation and immortal bliss,
for these are rather gifts of divine grace
through Christ and the Holy Spirit, who alone
can cure the human soul of its ills. He
distinguishes three grades of man's mental
state or powers — perception ($a\check{\iota}\sigma\theta\eta\sigma\iota s$), sight
($\check{o}\rho\alpha\sigma\iota s$), and illumination ($\phi\omega\tau\iota\sigma\mu\acute{o}s$). It is
the last through which the great secrets of the
divine are revealed.[77]

As concerns the resurrection and the life
hereafter, Macarius taught that the souls of
the righteous are raised to glory before their
bodies: apparently they pass at once to their
reward at physical death; but the bodies of all
are to rise on the great day, complete in every
member, not a hair missing; they will be bright
and shining with a divine effulgence. The
glory and the degree of happiness enjoyed by
each in paradise are to depend on the faith and
diligence that the individual has shown during
his earthly life. He who has attained to the
perfection of the Spirit will be free from all
distress and will enter wholly into an inex-

pressible union with the Spirit, so that the
human soul and the Holy Spirit will be one.
In Gehenna also many grades of punishment
await the wicked, fitted to their sins. Yet
Macarius nowhere suggests that punishment is
remedial or that the wicked can ever hope to
be purged and attain happiness, as Origen and
Gregory of Nyssa had done.[78]

In Macarius we find virtually no appeal to
human reason: he demands faith, not assent
to persuasive argument. His mysticism is
based directly on the Scriptures, but expressed
in the traditional language of Greek materialistic philosophy. Nor was this materialism
much in disaccord with the philosophic thought
of his time. His doctrine of the working of sin,
for example, which he held to be an act of
Satan, a power ($\pi\nu\epsilon\hat{v}\mu\alpha$) of finest matter, that
pervades the soul of man (also a $\pi\nu\epsilon\hat{v}\mu\alpha$) until
the two are one, as his view of the fusion of the
human soul with the Holy Spirit, could have
had little that was strange or objectionable to
the Neoplatonist, although the latter chose to
deal with the subject in different fashion; for
the Neoplatonist did not draw a clear line in
the lower grades of emanations between the
spiritual and the material: in fact, if we may

speak of exactitude in connection with mysticism, we may confidently say that Macarius is more exact in his thought than most of his contemporaries in that he clearly distinguished between the material and spiritual realms, holding that God alone is pure spirit while all else is material, and since he provided for the union of God and man through the incarnation of God, which was accomplished for the express purpose of effecting that union.

Neoplatonic mysticism became more and more the dominant element in the thought of the Eastern fathers, although here and there Aristotelian anthropological ideas were influential. On the whole rational arguments gave way before mystic imaginings and the way of faith was exalted over reasoned proof. The climax of this tendency, so to speak, is found in the works of the Pseudo-Dionysius the Areopagite, whose writings probably date from about the end of the fifth century. In them we find the later form of Neoplatonism, as represented by Proclus, freely put to the service of Christianity. The unknown author, to whom for convenience we shall refer hereafter simply as Dionysius, was a thoroughgoing mystic who attempted to combine with unwavering faith in the Holy Scriptures the explanations offered by that most mystic of philosophies as to the nature of God, His relation to the whole order of creation, and the salvation of the human soul.

God is described by Dionysius as the supreme and ultimate Unity, infinite and universal above all Being and Personality. Therefore he may not be spoken of as a Being or Essence, for these terms imply a personality, an individual existence; but an individual is a being distinguished from all other beings and in a sense separate from them, and therefore finite. God, as the ultimate Unity, includes within himself all things; yet we may not identify Him with any one of the things perceived by the senses or through the intelligence, although He is the cause of all and is to be found in all; in Him all things have their source, their beginning, for in Him dwell the ideas and models (ἰδέαι καὶ παραδείγματα) of all things; and in Him all find their end. Therefore this Christian mystic, like his Neoplatonic models, found all positive definitions of God inadequate: he could only say what God is not, and he well-nigh exhausts the vocabulary of negatives in his attempt to define the Deity.[79]

God is manifest in the Trinity, but how, is past man's power to explain: the fact is made known to us by revelation and must be accepted on faith. The Trinity also is to be regarded as supreme Unity, above all personality, above nature and all goodness of which man can conceive: it is the Lord (ἔφορος) of Christian theosophy, for it is by man's recognition of the mystery of the Trinity and by his worship of this Unity that he obtains knowledge of God and secures that divine wisdom which is eternal life.[80] But in spite of his reiterated emphasis of the unity of God and of the Trinity, Dionysius, like other Christian writers under the influence of Neoplatonism, is forced to abandon the monism that belongs to that philosophy since he draws an essential distinction between God and that which is not God.

To understand Dionysius it has been necessary to begin with his theology and on this we must dwell somewhat further. True to his philosophic predecessors, Dionysius held that God from the very exuberance of His being overflows by emanations into the infinite variety of invisible and visible creatures, illuminating all creations so that they share in his glory, even as each object in nature shares in the light of the sun according to its capacity. God's overflowing is eternally in two directions or streams, so to speak, which, however, are not independent or separate: one is in the direction of the Universal, the other toward the Particular. The former has an abstract existence or rather is an abstract idea of abstract existence; the latter is particular being which does not in reality exist: both are mere potentialities. The commingling of the particular stream with the universal is the process of creation; each created thing therefore we may say has two characters: one which makes it share in the infinite One, the other by virtue of which separate creatures come into being. Thus God is ever reaching down into the particular, passing from His transcendency above all being into the realm of the particular in which each creature has its own individuality of which we can make affirmative statements. This downward movement is what Dionysius, like Proclus before him, calls the affirmative way. Thus it is that we can say that everything exists in God; yet inasmuch as God transcends particular existence we can more truly define him by negative terms.[81]

All created things are substantially distinct from God, but since they owe whatever being they have to His goodness they are good. Therefore evil has no real existence in itself but exists only by participation in good: it is not inherent in things, it cannot come from God or exist in Him. Evil spirits even are not evil by nature: they have become so because they have not maintained the good state in which they were created, but have fallen away from goodness. In short, evil is a defect, a lack of goodness ($\sigma\tau\acute{\epsilon}\rho\eta\sigma\iota\varsigma$ $\dot{\alpha}\gamma\alpha\theta o\hat{v}$); it tends to reduce to nothingness whatever it affects; hence it must be itself nothing: it can have no substantial existence. If it had, the world would be dualistic in that it would have two original principles, which is impossible.

In God's sight the causes of evil are powers that work good: Providence uses those who have proved to be evil for their own or for the common advantage. Yet it will not force men against their will to be good, for it is foreign to Providence to do violence to nature: therefore men are allowed to act as free agents; and hence evil men are justly punished for their wrongdoings, since they have neglected to use the power of choice which is theirs.[82]

In what then does the salvation of man consist and how may it be accomplished? [83] Man's purpose and perfection are realized by his being made divine, that is, so far as may be, like God, and so one with Him. The divine love draws man upward towards his source; the good in man moves him to seek the Divine Good. That this may be accomplished the Ecclesiastical Hierarchy has been established, corresponding on earth to the Heavenly Hierarchy above through which God reveals himself to His creatures. The Hierarchy on earth is provided with many sensible symbols by aid of which man may be raised to God. The divine oracles, written and oral, direct man upward. The symbolic acts of the Church — baptism, communion, and consecration and use of the chrism — are all sacred mysteries which have a triple function: they purify, illuminate, and bestow a perfecting knowledge of divine actions by which in holy fashion the unifying elevation to the Supreme Being and the most blessed fellowship with Him are completed. The several orders of deacons, priests, and bishops have their own proper functions; and the initiates are divided into three groups, the first consisting of those who are being purified under the direction of deacons that they may participate in the sacraments; the second is made up of those who are receiving illumination under priests and who may partake of the divine symbols; but the highest group are those who, having been already purified and admitted to share in the divine mysteries by which they are illuminated, are being perfected under the charge of the bishops: of this class the monks are the first who by their pure service and devotion to God and their undivided and single life are fashioned into a certain God-like unity and perfection in that those elements in them which were once separate are brought into a sacred combination.

Thus the path of man's ascent to the divine may be accomplished. The symbols of the church aid him in the effort to which the natural good in him impels; he passes from the life of sensation to that of reason and thence to that of the spirit: in his upward course he turns away from outward things and seeks to return to the source whence he came: his way is the way of negation in that he rejects that which belonged and properly belonged to his lower stages. Thus the Finite returns to the Infinite, to the Absolute, and seeks to lose itself in union with God. As he mounts upward man acquires an increasing knowledge of God intellectually, for like is known by like; finally in ecstatic union with Him the perfect soul has that knowledge which is above all knowledge and which is eternal life. The finite self is again undifferentiated from the Infinite.[84]

Yet Dionysius will not allow that the finite soul thus absorbed in the Infinite loses its conscious individuality. He makes no attempt however to explain the paradox. The requirements of Christian faith forced the mystic to cling to this belief that personality must survive in the immortal soul.

In this Neoplatonic concept of God and His universe it was not easy to find a place for either divine grace or the redemptive work of Christ. The Platonic belief that the good in man naturally seeks the Divine Good from which it sprang logically would render both these elements otiose in Dionysius's plan. We must indeed recognize that grace plays no great part in his scheme. But concerning the nature of Christ he felt no difficulty in regarding Him as at once truly man, yet more than man; and in holding Him to be equally divine. But Christ's atoning work, according to his ideas, appears to be chiefly that of delivering man from the loss of his natural good through sin or error.[85] Of eschatological matters Dionysius has nothing to say. He paints no picture of Hell or Heaven.

In Dionysius Christian mysticism reached its earliest culmination. It was natural that his work should have great influence in the succeeding centuries. In the seventh the acute Maximus the Confessor († 662) through his commentaries on the four treatises contributed greatly to his master's popularity with a mystic age, and by his simple style and clarity of thought he made his predecessor's difficult works more intelligible and so more available for his successors. In the West about the middle of the ninth century John the Scot at the command of Charles the Bald translated into Latin the four treatises of Dionysius which had been sent to Louis the Pious by the Eastern emperor Michael Balbus in 827; and he also composed a commentary on them. In his work *De divisione Naturae* he bases his speculations on Dionysius but shows also the influence of Maximus, the two Gregories, and Augustine. In the first part of the twelfth century Hugo of St. Victor composed a commentary on the " Heavenly Hierarchy " in the Latin form given it by John the Scot, and approximately a century later Robert Grosseteste took time from his Aristotelian studies to translate and comment on the treatises " On the Divine Names " and on " Mystic Theology " and to revise John's translation of the two Hierarchies; and Albertus Magnus also found the rôle of commentator a congenial one. Thus the Dionysian Neoplatonism was transmitted and made part of the common thought of theologians. It remained for the mighty pupil of Albertus to incorporate this thought in the *Summa*. But to St. Thomas we shall come later.

VII. AUGUSTINE

WE MUST now turn back to the western half of the Mediterranean world. Here Christianity was predominantly Greek during the first three centuries: the church services were in Greek, the writers employed Greek, and for the most part Greek thought prevailed. Yet by the end of the second century the church in the West, at first in Africa, began to show a Latin individuality of its own and certain Roman characteristics gradually appeared: the Roman mind was legal and judicial rather than philosophic, and therefore tended to lay more weight on the gospel as a law, obedience to which set man right with God, rather than on the Greek view that man's mortal nature was saved by being made divine. It was Tertullian who created the Latin type, which was then advanced by Cyprian, Ambrose, and others. In their works more emphasis is laid on morality, on repentance for sin, both original and the wrong acts of the individual, and on divine grace than in the works of the Eastern fathers of the same time. We have already glanced at Tertullian's views on immortality. Significant as Cyprian and Ambrose are in the history of the Christian Church, we must pass them by and come at once to Augustine.[86]

Born at Tagaste in northern Africa of a pagan father and Christian mother, he devoted himself in his tempestuous early life to the study of rhetoric. The reading of Cicero's *Hortensius* turned him to the serious consideration of philosophy and religious matters, but it was not until 387 that he was baptized by Ambrose. This greatest of the Latin doctors, through long years of inner conflict and development, revealed the course of his thought in voluminous writings, beginning with his three books *Against the Academics* in 386, and closing with his *Retractationes* in A.D. 427. After his conversion to Christianity, he constantly dwelt on questions touching the nature and fate of the human soul, many of which he was forced to confess he found himself unable to solve.

Platonic writings, largely of the later schools and chiefly in the Latin translations of Victorius, showed Augustine the way by which he could accept Christianity as a reasonable religion, and the same philosophy provided him with a defense against the scepticism of the Academic School which had early attracted him, and the dualism of the Manichaeans to which he had been inclined for fully ten years. All his thought became permeated by later Platonism, which remained fundamental with him to the end. In this sense he is akin to the Platonizing Greek fathers and the mysticism of the East; but time, inheritance, and temper of mind made his theology as a whole different from that of Clement and Origen, as well as from that of the later Greek Fathers.

The knowledge of God and of the human soul was for Augustine his entire concern, for by this knowledge alone could he hope to attain perfect happiness: his reason would be satisfied only when it possessed the absolute Good — that is God himself.[87] To a discussion of the soul he devoted four special works written at different periods in his career: *De Immortalitate Animae,* 387; *De Quantitate Animae,* 387–388; *Epistola CLXVI ad Hieronimum,* 415; *De Anima et eius Origine,* 420. But scattered through many of the works are numerous pages that have important bearing on the theme with which he was so much concerned. Yet nowhere do we find any systematic and complete discussion of the soul. When we state Augustine's views briefly, and therefore of necessity in schematic fashion, we are, in a sense, misrepresenting him, for his ideas changed in the course of his life, while on certain points he never arrived at clear convictions.

Being a Platonist, Augustine could not regard the human soul as corporeal and material, as many Christian thinkers held, but he steadfastly maintained that the soul is a spirit. He argued that every body has spatial extension: it can be measured and of it we form an image; it does not subsist in and by itself but inheres in some subject. The soul, on the contrary, is without spatial extension: it is a substance in the Aristotelian sense; it requires no subject in which it may inhere, but subsists by itself. The soul can know itself not only by external signs but directly by an act of pure intelligence. If the soul were corporeal as the body is, it could not have such direct knowledge of itself but would be reduced to certain opinions concerning its own nature, which indeed are the most that anyone can have of his own body, for the mind is forced to judge of the body by external signs, by the way the body acts; but the soul can have knowledge of itself directly, and therefore can have a more perfect knowledge of its own nature than of anything else in the world. Such direct knowledge was for Augustine, as for all Platonists, certain proof of the soul's spirituality. As consciousness witnesses to the existence of the soul, so all the faculties of thinking, knowing, willing, remembering, judging, show the soul's true nature. Moreover, if the soul were corporeal, it could give us knowledge of itself only through the senses, that is to say, knowledge of corporeal things; but the soul is the means by which we know incorporeal things, like abstractions; therefore the soul must itself be incorporeal.

The best definition of the human soul that he formulates is that it is a certain substance which participates in reason and is suited to directing the body: it is that which vivifies the body, that without which the body is dead; on it depends all sensual perception, and it includes as its highest functions memory, will, and intelligence, which have no existence apart from the soul, but are identical with it — they are three relatively but one substantially.

In his definition of the whole man Augustine's fidelity to the sacred tradition forced him to part company with the Platonists. For the latter held, as we have seen above, to a dualistic doctrine which saw only in the soul, or at least in the reasoning part of the soul, the true man, and which regarded the body as the hampering abode or tomb of the soul. But Augustine, throughout his maturer years, held that body as well as soul was needed to make up the complete man: in fact, that these two elements are inseparable — without both, human personality cannot exist. Nor could he regard the human soul simply as part of a universal soul. Although he had debated this question in his earlier years, he seems to have become convinced that each soul is an individual entity. Even more impossible did he find it to believe that the soul of man participates in the soul of God, as the Alexandrian Platonists, the Manichaeans, and others maintained. It appeared to him that if that were true, God would not be perfect and unchanging, for we know that the human soul lacks perfection and suffers change.[88]

Inasmuch as Augustine held that both body and soul were needed to make up a human personality, it followed for him that the whole man, not his soul alone, must be capable of immortality and unending happiness. This belief was assured him by faith, not by any human argument.[89] In this position he showed himself a true son of the church and faithful heir to the Christian tradition. Nevertheless, he offered certain interesting proofs of immortality which show him equally a debtor to the Platonic line.

Plotinus had declared that since man's soul thinks the absolute essences, whether because it finds within itself such concepts or remembers them, it clearly existed before the body; and that since it possesses this eternal knowledge, it must be eternal itself.[90] Augustine could not accept the theory that the soul had had an existence anterior to that in the body, an existence from which it remembered the eternal ideal, for his faith in the Scriptures required him to believe that the human soul was created by God and had not emanated from Himself. Many, like the Neoplatonists, the Gnostics, the Manichaeans, and others, held to the theory of emanation, but Augustine, after much consideration of certain passages in the *Old Testament,* became convinced that the souls of the first man and the first woman were created by God from nothing; but he could never decide whether these acts of creation had been performed at the beginning or on the sixth day; nor could he decide when the souls of our first parents entered their bodies. He was likewise unable to determine how the souls of the descendants of Adam and Eve came into being; but, on the whole, he was rather inclined to the view that souls are descended from the soul of the first man even as bodies descend through the parents by generation. This theory commended itself to him as being more in accord with Scripture and with orthodox belief than other hypotheses, and it explained the sufferings of the apparently innocent by showing the way in which original sin could be inherited.[91]

One thing that early supported Augustine in his faith in immortality was that Truth exists in the soul and testifies to man of its existence there. But Truth is an inseparable attribute of the soul; it must then follow that since the attribute cannot exist longer than the subject to which it belongs, and since Truth, the attribute, is immortal, the soul, the subject, must also be immortal. A similar argument he found in the fact that Knowledge too belongs to the soul. Now Knowledge is knowledge of some science: but Science is immortal; therefore the soul cannot come to an end. Moreover, the soul is the seat of Reason which cannot be separated from it any more than Truth and Knowledge. Consequently, since Reason is immortal, the soul must likewise be.[92]

The Platonic character of these arguments is self-evident. A further proof he borrows bodily from Plato's *Phaedo* and from Plotinus, when he maintains that life and the soul are identical, whereas the body is animated not by itself but by its soul. The body, therefore, can die — that is, be deprived of life; but the soul, whose essence is life, cannot lose that essence, cannot desert itself, and therefore cannot die.[93]

The defects inherent in these arguments were not unknown to Augustine and caused him much debate with himself. In later years he found the most convincing evidence of man's immortality in the soul's inborn passion for it, which differs from the instinct that prompts even the irrational animals to shrink from death in that man's longing is based on reason. We must believe, therefore, that this longing comes from God; consequently, it will be satisfied only by the attainment of immortality. Closely allied to this is man's natural longing for happiness; but complete happiness, in Augustine's view, can only be attained by attaining the supreme Good — that is, God; and since man cannot possess God in this life, another life is needed and a life that will be without end; for the possession of the supreme Good for a limited time will not give satisfaction; therefore we must believe in immortality: cum ergo beati esse omnes homines velint, si vere volunt, profecto et esse immortales volunt; aliter enim beati esse non possent.[94]

Yet all his arguments failed to satisfy Augustine. He was keenly conscious of the objections that could be raised against them, and much as he depended on Plotinus and the great teacher, Plato, in his old age he found his proofs obscure and fell back constantly on the tradition of the church and on Christian faith. The great fact for him remained that Christ put on mortality that we might, in our turn, share in that immortality which Christ alone can bestow: Si enim natura Dei filius propter filios hominum misericordia factus est hominis filius; hoc est enim, *Verbum caro factum est et habitavit in nobis* hominibus: quanto est credibilius, natura filios hominis gratia Dei filios Dei fieri, et habitare in Deo, in quo solo et de quo solo esse possunt beati participes immortalitatis eius effecti; propter quod persuadendum Dei filius particeps nostrae mortalitatis effectus est? [95]

Augustine, however, did not believe that man of his own effort, whether through faith or works, could win immortality for himself. Faithful to the apostle's doctrine, he held that " in Adam's fall we sinned all ": through pride our first progenitor lost the happy communion with God and forfeited His grace which he originally enjoyed, lapsing into a hopeless moral state the end of which would properly be the everlasting death of the soul; and all of Adam's descendants share in that sin. From this original sin, as from the sins done in the flesh, only the grace of God can save man; and this grace is a free gift bestowed, like all other things, not as something earned, but solely as God chooses to give it: He predestinates whom He will for punishment and for salvation. Augustine in his maturer years did not concede that man had power to accept or reject God's grace, but held that it is irresistible: that through it the individual is inspired with faith and filled with love for the right, so that his nature is transformed and he is enabled to persist in righteousness. Moreover he believed that the sacraments of the Catholic Church were holy symbols and instruments without which man could not secure entrance into the kingdom of God or obtain salvation and everlasting life. He thus may fairly be called the father of the doctrine of predestination, which, often in fearful forms, has been held down to our own time; by his belief in original sin he helped to fix that baneful idea among the tenets of the church; and through his emphasis on the value of the sacraments as essential instruments, possessed solely by the Church, he contributed mightily to the doctrine that the orthodox Catholic Church was the sole channel through which salvation could be secured.

As to the future state of the soul, Augustine naturally was obliged to reject those cyclical views which were expressed in the Platonic-Orphic doctrines of palingenesis and metempsychosis. He did not claim to have seen beyond the veil so clearly that he could speak with any certainty, but he evidently felt that when the soul was separated from the earthly body by death, it continued for a time without even an ethereal body, and, being incorporeal, could not be occupying any extended space but rather some place similar to extended space, or perhaps wholly unextended. There it was to suffer the hell which each has within his own soul — spiritual punishments for the sins of this life; and it was destined to know spiritual joys far transcending any known to corporeal life. At the resurrection the souls would receive their spiritual bodies, and in some regions unknown to us would receive unending joys or punishments. He thought it possible that the bodies of the damned would be composed of thick and humid air, so that they would suffer from the physical fire of hell; or if their bodies were to be spiritual, he found it as easy to believe that these bodies would suffer when united with fire as it was to understand the union of soul and body on earth. But the righteous, in their spiritual bodies, beautiful beyond all earthly beauty, would enjoy inexpressible happiness: they were to live at peace and in obedience to God, with never-ending joy. Their happiness would vary in degree, it is true, but all would be satisfied: the pure in heart would see God.[96]

VIII. SUMMARY OF GREEK PHILOSOPHIC INFLUENCES

AT THIS point it may be well to summarize briefly the Greek philosophic influences that were potent in shaping Christian thought throughout antiquity and the middle ages. The three philosophic systems which were most significant were Platonism, Aristotelianism, and Stoicism; Epicureanism we may here disregard. Stoicism was a materialistic monism, Platonism an idealistic dualism. Neither had preserved its original character inviolate: the former, eclectic in its origin, had been deeply influenced by the latter before the beginning of the Christian era; yet it had maintained unimpaired its belief that the World-soul, God, and the human soul, although made of the finest and most subtle matter, were alike material no less than the stones that lie in man's path. Moreover, Stoicism had never come to believe that even the noblest could look forward to an endless life of future happiness, in spite of the noble picture of the rewards of those who have deserved the best of their fellows and their state, which we can still see in Cicero's *Dream of Scipio;* but through the fortifying power of its noble ethics, this philosophy commended itself to those who confessed the Christian faith; while its materialistic explanation of the soul was far from being discordant with the ideas that had come into Christianity from Judaism, and which were easy for those who held that the body, no less than the soul, was an essential element in the individual's personality.

Again the Stoic doctrine of the immanence of God, in accord with which man's soul must be regarded as a part of the World-soul, which pervades and animates all things, agreed with much Christian thinking, and is not far from certain modern beliefs. Furthermore this view of the relation of the individual soul to the all-pervading World-soul had as its corollary a belief in the essential brotherhood of men, whence followed the conclusion that merit depends not on position but on well doing. These views were welcome to the thoughtful Christian and had an effect on the views of the Church.

The greatest contribution of Stoicism, however, was in the field of practical ethics. The

Stoic not only laid great emphasis on the training of the will under the direction of reason, but he also formulated practical rules for the moral edification of one's self. The early Stoics held that man's moral nature could in a moment be completely changed to a state of perfection, and doctrinaire members of the later school continued to cherish this view; but by the beginning of our era the facts of human nature had modified the general doctrine from that of instantaneous conversion to that of a gradual advance in virtue, which must be secured by constant effort. Both positions have their analogies in Christian doctrine, even to the present day.

Yet it remains true that we can adduce comparatively few concrete examples of the direct influence of Stoicism on the Church Fathers and the Schoolmen. The explanation is to be found in the fact that Stoic doctrines on the subjects named early became the common property of thinkers, and therefore formed a part of the Christian inheritance.

In Plato's own thought the transcendence of God is always at least implicit, and by his followers it is clearly expressed. To bridge the gap between the transcendent Deity and the created world, later Platonists resorted to systems of emanations, often elaborate and fanciful; but these very systems seemed to furnish a basis for the doctrine of the Triune God, when the necessity arose of defining the relation of the Father, Son, and Holy Spirit. Again Platonism had from the first emphasized the incorporeal, spiritual nature of the soul, and had regarded the material body as a clogging element which hampers its spiritual inhabitant in its effort to live the divine life that is its by nature, for the soul is akin to the Divine. Being thus akin, the human soul naturally seeks to return to God and to be at home with Him. Divinity and immortality are one in Plato's thought and in that of many after him. We have already seen that certain Christian writers welcomed such a concept.

Moreover Plato held that the soul's growth while imprisoned in the body is to be furthered by the subjection of that body, allowing the soul to have as little commerce as possible with its temporal abode: the true philosopher, like St. Paul, must die daily to the body and its passions, or as Plato puts it, " practise death and dying." The meaning of this is made clear by Socrates's words in the *Theaetetus:* " We ought to fly away from earth to heaven as quickly as possible, and to fly away is to become like God, so far as we are able and to become like him is to become holy, just, and wise." This doctrine of a noble asceticism made a strong appeal to many Christian thinkers, and was influential in the development of Christian asceticism.

Although Plato nowhere gives us a clear apocalyptic vision of the ultimate fate of the pure soul, in spite of his myths that hint at the nature of the future life, his later followers, seizing on the mystic strain in the master's thought, developed the doctrine that the ultimate reward of the purest souls is to be found in the vision of God Himself, wherein will be given all knowledge and perfect bliss without end. It is not strange that the Church Fathers adopted this as the supreme joy of the Saints.

We can then readily understand why Platonism in its later forms was for many centuries the dominant philosophic element in Christian metaphysics, both East and West, although it had to be modified at numerous points to meet the requirements of Christian faith.

There were, however, things in Platonism that pressed the Christians hard when they tried to reconcile their philosophic lessons with certain elements in the well-established Christian tradition. Plato, for instance, had not hesitated to say that since the soul of man is immortal, it must have existed from eternity, — that is, that it is eternal; but such a view is diametrically opposed to the account of creation in *Genesis* and to the long-cherished views of the church. Again, if the body and soul are opposed in nature, the one material and mortal, the other spiritual and divine, so that the soul is the real man and the body only his imperfect and temporary habitation, how can it be that the body shall be raised and have an endless existence as the dwelling place of the immortal soul? St. Paul's explanation might be accepted as a comfort to one's faith, but the logic of the explanation was still defective; equally difficult was the doctrine of punishment by fire. Some, like Origen, courageously sought a way out of their difficulties by symbolism and allegory, but the majority at this point abandoned Platonism in favor of the sacred tradition.

Aristotle, in comparison with his teacher, was neglected in later antiquity. It is true that his works had been a subject of learned study from an early date, but it was not until the sixth century that his philosophy began to have a clear influence on Christian thought. This influence in the West was almost wholly due to Boethius († 525), who by his translations of the *Categories* and the *De interpretatione,* and by his commentaries and his treatises on logic, disclosed to his successors the Aristotelian method and logic, as well as furnished them with a summary of the Aristotelian ontology. Henceforth many of the early Scholastics drew indirectly on the treasures of the Peripatetic School. Both the form and to a certain extent the content of mediaeval philosophy became more and more Aristotelian; yet down to the middle of the thirteenth century Aristotelian studies proper were virtually confined to Greeks, Arabs, and Syrians.

Aristotelianism had numerous elements that fitted well with Christian thought and speculation. For example its theistic character provided philosophic arguments for the existence of God more convincing than those which any form of Platonism offered to the logical mind. Again Aristotle's concept of man as a living unit, in which body and soul combine to make a whole, accorded with the traditional Christian concept of the person. In Aristotelian thought both soul and body are necessary, each to the other: the material body by itself has only the potentiality of life; the soul makes that potentiality actual. Again in Aristotelian psychology it is the body which through the senses arouses the feelings that determine the individual's movements and provide the bases of his memory as of his knowledge of the external world; and finally it is through the noblest part of his soul that man reasons and creates his conceptual world. The body then is the material condition of the soul's activities, and the soul is the "perfection," the "fulfillment," of the body. Therefore Aristotle found it difficult to think of a human soul as existing apart from its body.

Thus Christian thinkers could find comfort and philosophic support for their belief in the resurrection of the body; furthermore by a somewhat distorted interpretation of Aristotle's statement that the active reason is alone divine and comes to man "from without," Church Fathers and Schoolmen were confirmed in their view that each rational soul is specially created by God and infused into man either at conception or at some later moment in his foetal life.

However, it was not until the twelfth and thirteenth centuries that Aristotle's major works began to be directly known in the West: in 1128 the *Topics* and the *Analytics* were translated into Latin; early in the next century the *Physics* and the *Metaphysics* were made available, and shortly thereafter the *De anima,* the *Ethics,* and the *Politics.* The credit of turning scholastic thought definitely to Aristotle belongs chiefly to Albertus Magnus (1193–1280) and to his great pupil, Thomas Aquinas (1225–1274): in fact we may almost say without exaggeration that the latter not only first, but finally, put peripatetic philosophy fully at the service of Christian theology.

IX. THOMAS AQUINAS

THIS IS not the place to review at length the life and activities of Thomas Aquinas, but his importance requires that some brief account of him be given. He was fortunate in his training and in his intellectual relations throughout. Born of a noble family at Aquino in 1225 he began his education in his fifth year at Monte Cassino, whence he went to Naples to continue his studies. There he entered the Dominican order about 1244. The following year was of the greatest significance in his development, for on going to Paris he became a pupil of Albertus Magnus who gave him that interest in Aristotelian philosophy which was to dominate his own thought for the rest of his life, and which through him was destined to be potent in the greater part of the Church down to the present day. In 1248 he accompanied his master to Cologne; but four years later he returned to Paris to complete his studies for the degree of Master in Theology (1256) and to lecture there until 1259. By this time his learning and power as a teacher had made him widely known, so that he was called to be a professor in the *studium curiae* at the Papal Court, residing first at Anagni and later at Orvieto; in 1265 he became director of studies at Santa Sabina in Rome, but after two years he rejoined the Papal Court at Viterbo. Early in 1269, however, doctrinal strife caused him to be returned to Paris to combat Averroism and to oppose certain attacks on the mendicant orders; three years later he went back to Naples, whence he was summoned early in 1274 by Pope Gregory X to attend the council at Lyons; but early in his journey he fell sick and died on March 7 at the Abbey of Fossanova.[97]

In spite of his constant activity as teacher Thomas found time to compose a great number of commentaries, doctrinal treatises, and systematic works, to which theologians, and many others as well, have been indebted down to our own day. The range of his reading was enormous and his mind was one of the ablest ever possessed by man. He made his first acquaintance with Aristotle while a student at Naples; from Albertus Magnus he derived much, as we have just stated; but his thorough knowledge was gained largely through the Latin translations or revisions of William of Moerbeke, his contemporary and fellow Dominican, with whom he became acquainted during his first residence at the Papal Court. From his study of these translations he gained habits of clear and logical thought as well as provided himself with reasonable arguments to support his faith. By his own commentaries, which displayed a new method of interpretation, he gained recognition as the chief expositor of Aristotelianism.

With Plato he had little direct acquaintance; but from St. Augustine he learnt much of later Platonism, as he did from Chalcidius, Boethius, Proclus (in William of Moerbeke's translation), Pseudo-Dionysius, and the *liber de causis*, which became widely known and influential after the middle of the thirteenth century. He was acquainted also with the Jewish and Arabian writers, especially with Maimonides and Avencebrol; and his knowledge of the Church Fathers and earlier Scholastics was profound.

Of Thomas's many works the ones with which we are chiefly concerned are his *Summa de veritate catholicae fidei contra gentiles* written between 1259–1264 to combat Arabian scholars chiefly, and his *Summa Theologiae*, begun in 1265 and left unfinished at his death. These must be supplemented at certain points by other writings, especially by his *Quaestiones disputatae* and *quodlibetales*.

Thomas Aquinas was the first to treat systematically the relations of faith and reason, and of theology and philosophy. Thereby he established the two constructive methods of scholastic philosophy: authority and apologetics.[98] We must briefly consider his views on the relation of these two and on kindred matters first, for they are fundamental to his doctrines concerning the soul and its future states.

As a true disciple of Aristotle Thomas held that the human mind can penetrate beyond the sensible and phenomenal world and understand the very essence of things, can grasp Being itself, for in a certain sense, that is potentially, man is wholly being; and he maintained that the human intellect has the power to receive all intelligible forms, as his senses can receive all sensible forms. Therefore the intellect can comprehend the existence of supersensible existences. This claim is based on his theory of knowledge, the principle of which is stated more than once: " quidquid recipitur, recipitur per modum recipientis "; again " cognitum est in cognoscente per modum cognoscentis "; that is, " like is known by like." Therefore as the bodily senses are akin to matter, so the human reason is related to immaterial existences. Moreover he steadfastly maintains that the subjective modifications of the intellect, the concepts formed by it, are not the direct objects of our thought, but merely the means by which we know the external reality to which they correspond. It follows then that our knowledge is not simply subjective, but that it rather deals with objective reality and therefore can be trusted.[99] These are the matters with which Philosophy is concerned.

Yet there are truths which are too lofty for human reason, truths which belong to the supernatural realm and which can be known only through faith and revelation. Such themes belong to Theology: it is concerned first of all with God, and secondarily with such matters as the Trinity, the incarnation, sacraments, original sin, purgatory, resurrection of the body, judgment, eternal joy and punishment. These are subjects which can never be adequately dealt with by reason alone, but must be accepted by man through the action of his will.[100] Not that philosophy and theology are opposed to each other or in any discord: on the contrary they are at one, but the former cannot mount to the realm that belongs to the latter; yet reason can support theology, provided that first, moved by an impulse from God and from the evidences found in the external world, the reasoner recognizes and believes in the divine revelation. For example, human reason can prove the existence of God. In fact Thomas offers five proofs of His existence, the Aristotelian origin of most of which is evident at a glance.[101] Yet although human reason can by itself prove that God exists and that he is one, and can establish other facts of the same class concerning Him, we still must recognize that all such proofs are based on sensible experience of the eternal corporeal world. But sensible experience can tell us nothing of God's essential nature: that nature we can know only from revelation, which tells us that God is simple Unity, pure Being in Himself, transcendent, perfect, and infinite; He is his own essence, and in Him Essence, Intelligence, Will, and Truth are one; He is his own eternal life and enjoys perfect happiness. He is not, however, the universal abstraction of the Neoplatonists, but is an uncreated Person, uniting in himself the perfection of all Being. God created the cosmos from nothing, and He secures its conservation by continuous creation. At this point Thomas departs from Aristotle, who held that the cosmos was eternal; but the doctrine of creation in time is for Thomas wholly an article of faith; it is not capable of logical proof.[102] In Thomas's view, although all beings owe their existence to God, they are not lost in Him, for each is an individual. In fact the great scholastic holds with Aristotle that every being which exists or which can exist, other than the abstractions of the mind, is distinct from every other being, that is, each being is a substance: he follows his teacher so faithfully that he emphatically declares more than once that the individual is the only thing that exists at all (nihil est praeter individuum). Therefore he is at this point a pluralist.

The individual consists of matter and form: prime matter is an incomplete element of reality; it is a passive potentiality, distinct from form; but it cannot exist apart from form, for the undetermined cannot be. Form is that which gives being, substantiality, to a body. The principle of individualization is matter, which, limited and defined spatially (materia signata), receives its appropriate form.[103]

The soul is man's form. It is not complex, but simple, single, not tripartite as Plato had held. It is the first principle of man's life and activity, at once the efficient, formal, and final cause of his being. It possesses the three functions described by Aristotle, namely the vegetative, appetitive, and intellectual or rational. The first two are earlier in time and form the embryo, while the rational function, the Aristotelian νοῦς, is a direct creation which combines the two others with itself so that they lose their independence and are made subject, so to speak, to the rational. As the soul is the first principle of man, it must be incorporeal, for bodies, being material, do not have life and activity in themselves. The soul then is the first actuality (the Aristotelian entelechy) of the body.

Again the soul's immateriality is shown by the fact that the range of its activities is not physically limited, as it would be if it were corporeal. A corporeal nature would impose physical limitations and hamper the mind. The mind, however, is subject to no such restraints; it has activities in which the body has no share: it can reflect upon itself and its own activities, and can know the essences of things. It is true, of course, that the rational soul uses the body in such a way that it displays those characteristics which led Aristotle to postulate three souls; but the vegetative and the appetitive functions require the body for their action, whereas the reason, the active intellect, is independent of the body. Moreover, this active intellect is a substance in itself, since its action does not require the body. The possession of this intellect sets man apart from all the lower forms of life, which have vegetative and, if endowed with sensory activities, appetitive functions as well. Man alone can think and reflect on his own thoughts; and this activity requires no bodily organs. The human soul then must be immortal, for it is an immaterial substance, a subsistent form in itself; and a form cannot be separated from itself. Finally we should observe that Thomas adduces the ancient and persistent psychological argument that man's natural longing for immortality cannot be in vain.

Yet Thomas refuses to agree with Plato that the souls of men have existed eternally. They are rather for him individual creations of God, the intellectual function, as has been said above, being created at the end of human generation. Although Thomas maintained that the soul can exist apart from the body, he was insistent that both body and soul are necessary to make the complete man.

All men naturally seek happiness as their final end; but complete happiness can be nothing less than the vision of the Divine Essence, of God. Through that vision man becomes a participant in eternal life; in it all his desires are fulfilled; and it remains his forever. By his effort to attain this end man is distinguished from all other creatures. The effort calls for the exercise of man's noblest part, the intellect, directing the will; for to obtain this blessed state man must act morally, seeking always the Good, which attracts the will; but man's will is ever free to choose the better or the baser course; his reason offers to the will the proper motives for action and fit objects at which it should aim, thereby securing for man freedom. Moreover above man is God, who by His laws directs and sanctions man's acts, and by His grace lifts him upward, inclines him to the right, and secures for him forgiveness of sins.[104]

In Thomas's system the incarnation of Christ has an important place; indeed he enumerates no less than seven ways in which the incarnation aids man in his efforts to obtain complete and final happiness. First of all the incarnation brings man hope, since God, by uniting a human nature with himself once for all showed clearly that man, under the direction of his reason operating on his will, may be united with God and may see Him directly; again the incarnation teaches men to reject all lower aims and to seek the knowledge of God above all other things; and thirdly, through the incarnation God gives men direct and full assurance that their faith is true and to be trusted; fourthly, God thereby shows his love for man; fifthly, the incarnation provides an example of the truth that happiness is the reward of virtue; sixth, it secures for men remission of their sins and gives them assurance that such remission had been made; finally it furnishes satisfaction. And further by Christ's death all men who eagerly strive to be united with him are assured of salvation. The sacraments are the means (*remedia*) by which the benefits of His death are secured.[105]

The fate of man's immortal soul after death is fully determined by his life on earth: the soul of the good man has gained an unchangeable will to seek the good, as that of the evil man is set toward evil. Each individual soul is judged at once on separation from its terrestrial body. Those that are so defiled by sins that they cannot be cleansed and fitted for final happiness begin their endless punishment at once; the righteous few who are free from sin enter directly on their reward in Paradise; but the great majority are afflicted with sins from which they must be purified before they can be raised to the bliss that is to be finally theirs. These souls remain in purgatory until their sins have been burned away with fire, for God has power to make the incorporeal suffer from corporeal flames.

For the second and final judgment all will rise and present themselves before the great Judge. Each soul will now receive back its body, for both body and soul are necessary for the complete man; but the body, although composed of flesh and bones, will then be eternally incorruptible. The bodies of the righteous will be subject to their souls which will wholly rule their bodies' feelings and actions; these bodies will not know weakness or defect; they will be free from every evil, and with their souls will share in the celestial glories. The blessed will dwell forever with Christ above the heavens; they alone will perceive His divine nature, and in that vision they will find their complete joy.

The incorruptible bodies of the damned likewise will be wholly servants of their souls, which, having turned away from God toward carnal things, will make their bodies heavy, opaque, subject to sensory impressions and therefore capable of physical suffering. In the depths these carnal bodies, being incorruptible, will forever suffer everburning fire, according to their deserts; indeed not the carnal bodies alone, but the evil souls likewise must endure their distress, even as they now suffer corporeal fire in purgatory. Moreover, although Christ will appear to the evil as well as to the good at the final judgment, the wicked will not have power to discern his divine nature: they shall forever be deprived of the Beatific Vision. After the final judgment there shall be no more generation or death; the movements of the heaven shall cease; and both earth and heaven shall be cleansed with fire that the new heaven and the new earth of the Apocalypse may be established.[106]

Thomas Aquinas thus built up a unified logical system, cogent in its form and content; by his extraordinary critical power he was able to distinguish clearly between the essential and relevant and the non-essential and irrelevant; he left aside all that was useless or illogical, simplifying his arguments and thus giving strength to his conclusions. As we have already said, he established Aristotelianism as the chief foundation of Christian philosophy; but in his eschatological doctrine he returned to Neoplatonic mysticism and speculation. Elsewhere also he was often far from rejecting the views of later Platonism, but preferred to modify or reconcile them into his system; he treated in the same way Arabic and Jewish thought.

But his system was not by any means accepted by all, nor was Platonism driven from the field. Three years after his death certain of his doctrines were condemned by the bishop of Paris and the authorities of Oxford took similar action at almost the same time. The chief criticism of Thomism came from the rival order of the Franciscans, of whom the most famous was Duns Scotus († 1308), while the Dominicans ardently defended their brother. But since their controversies for the most part dealt with other questions than those touching the nature and the immortality of the soul, we need not review them now. It is sufficient to note that proof of the great influence of Thomas's work soon after his death is given by Dante's use of his philosophy and theology in his *Divina Commedia*, and by the place accorded the great Dominican in Christian art.[107] In the Western Church Thomism has been continuously potent to the present day; and its preëminent place in the Roman communion was finally recognized when Pope Leo XIII in 1879 ordained that the *Summa Theologiae* should be the basis of theological study.

X. CHRISTIAN MYSTICS. THE MODERN PERIOD

THE MYSTIC element in religion is large: the religious emotions are not content with logic alone. In Plato's thought and in the systems that his followers elaborated after him there are mystic strains that satisfy where closeknit reasoning fails. Therefore Platonism in one form or another has answered to the need of Christian mystics and has been strong in every age of Christian mysticism.

Such an era began in the twelfth century. It was inaugurated by Bernard of Clairvaux who revived the Augustinian doctrine of contemplation. For him humility and that love of God which springs therefrom are the means by which man may obtain knowledge of the truth: the two steps — first, thought, and second, contemplation culminating in ecstasy, lead the devout to his supreme goal where his soul is united with God and loses itself in Him, and in that union finds its complete joy.[108]

Bonaventura († 1274) also deserves mention for the strong mystic elements in his teachings; and we have just seen how Thomas Aquinas himself becomes essentially a Neoplatonist when he describes the final reward of the blessed.

In Germany a great mystic movement was inaugurated by Eckhart at the beginning of the fourteenth century; thence it spread to Switzerland and to the Netherlands. One of its products, the so-called " German Theology," was to influence Luther deeply, while another, the "Imitation of Christ" by Thomas à Kempis, is known to Christians everywhere. Again a wave of mysticism arose in connection with the Catholic revival of the sixteenth century, starting in Spain and spreading to Geneva and thence to France. In all these movements the aim was to attain in virtually Neoplatonic fashion an inner revelation through ecstasy and to secure a union of the human soul with God.

Moreover in northern Europe toward the end of the fifteenth century a marked tendency to return to the Neoplatonic ideas of Augustine had become manifest. This movement, starting at Paris, soon reached the newly founded

German universities. It was part of that humanistic revival which was now spreading from Italy to the North, and which was one of the precursors of the Protestant Reformation. The fifteenth century in Italy saw also the development of a secular culture in which Platonism and Neoplatonism played an important part; its devotees, however, were more concerned with this life than with thoughts of any future existence. Yet in this same period a vigorous defence of Aristotelianism against the Platonists arose, made by the antischolastics, both among the religious and non-religious alike, some following the commentaries of Averroes, others preferring the interpretations of Alexander of Aphrodisias. The Averroists, while affirming the unity and the eternity of the human intellect, denied the immortality of the individual soul; the Alexandrists insisted that the human soul perished with the body. The scholastics also still clung to Aristotle, but by their failure to adjust their teachings to the rapidly expanding thought of their time they ultimately confirmed their own decline.

The leaders of the Protestant Reformation exhibited a variety of philosophic tendencies in their dogmatic systems. Martin Luther, although he was no philosopher, had been early influenced by Augustine's mysticism, which appealed to him profoundly; but the center of Luther's doctrine was justification by faith rather than philosophic dogma. Yet his hostility to scholasticism made him an opponent of Aristotelianism in particular. Zwingli, in Switzerland, was led by his humanistic interests to employ Neoplatonic and Stoic principles in the formation of his theology; while. Melanchthon brought Aristotelianism into the permanent service of Protestantism in that he, like the great scholastics, employed the peripatetic system as a supplement to faith, maintaining that both faith and reason taught the same truths in different degrees.

By the seventeenth century the modern period of European philosophy had begun: the enlarged outlook and the freedom of the mind produced by attempts to realize again the life of the ancient Romans and Greeks, by scientific discoveries and geographical explorations, and by the many other influences operating in that movement which we call the Renaissance, required a new philosophy to explain the enlarged cosmos and to define man's present and future relation to it. Into the philosophic systems of the last three centuries we may not now penetrate or review in any detail even the views that have been advanced concerning the nature of the soul and its probable immortality, for these subjects are too vast and complex for any brief treatment. We can only indicate some tendencies in modern thought and suggest the relations of some more recent views to those of antiquity.

The position of the Christian Church has naturally been conditioned largely by regard for the *Old* and *New Testaments* and by the traditional dogmas long accepted by the majority of both Roman and Protestant Communions. In the Roman Church Thomism, with its philosophic bases of Aristotelianism and Neoplatonism, has been on the whole predominant during this latest period, and since 1879 has been officially recognized as the foundation of theology. This fact is far from meaning that Roman Catholic thinkers have been unconscious of the philosophic movements of the past three centuries or uninfluenced by them. As regards our special subject, however, modern Catholic scholars have had little difficulty in maintaining the essential principles of the Thomistic psychology and eschatology in satisfactory accord with the results of modern investigations and theories, or in the face of them. Since the Protestant branches have no such official theology everywhere established, greater variety of belief is found among its representatives, who often display more plainly the influence of modern philosophic speculation.

It is hardly necessary to say that the ancient Orphic-Pythagorean belief in palingenesis, that series of lives and deaths by which man is to be cleansed from his inherent sin, has found as little favor with Western thinkers in modern as in mediaeval times; but it is noteworthy that the so-called Christian doctrine of " original sin " that had so much essential kinship with the Greek concept is receiving less and less attention in our time, or is being quite disregarded in favor of modern views as to the source and nature of wrong action. The Platonic concept that the human soul is uncreated in time but has an eternal existence, early came into conflict with the Christian view that the soul of Adam was a direct creation by God; and that the souls of Adam's descendants were either inherited from him like their bodies or were individual creations at the time of conception, which were the two common mediaeval views. In modern times secular thinkers at least have for the most part discarded all these doctrines in the senses in which they were originally held; but philosophers who like McTaggart hold that the " self " is " a fundamental differentiation of the Absolute " should logically maintain that the " self," the " soul," is eternal. This, however, does not necessarily mean that the self has eternal self-consciousness or that it can at any given time look forward to a conscious immortality. Finally there is a modern view of the human soul as a separate development or creation which is closely connected with the doctrine of " conditional immortality " of which we must take note below. Aristotle had said that man only lives when he uses his reason; if he does not use his reason he is dead. Beginning with Henry Dodwell, whose treatise entitled *An Epistolary Discourse proving from the Scriptures and the first Fathers that the Soul is a Principle naturally mortal*, etc., was the first modern treatment of the subject (1706), some, shifting the emphasis from reason, have held that the " soul " is naturally mortal, but may be made capable of immortality through sacrament or other means of grace; or, as later and non-theological thinkers prefer to put the matter, the " soul " or " self " is a development within each man, a unity made by persistent moral purpose and upright action, the aims of which extend beyond the grave. Such selves, created by purposeful effort, alone possess life, and are worthy of immortality. Naturally the strict followers of tradition will have none of such doctrine.

When we consider modern attempts to describe the soul itself we observe that the definition of the soul as a simple substance and therefore immortal, which the scholastics developed chiefly from Aristotelianism, is today abandoned or greatly modified by many thinkers not connected with the Roman Communion. Within that body the term is maintained for whatever exists *per se,* and therefore it is employed to describe the soul or mind, which is defined " as the subject of our mental life, the ultimate principle by which we feel, think, and will." [109] Yet modern secular philosophers have not wholly abandoned the notion of substantiality. In the seventeenth century Descartes, Spinoza, Leibnitz, and Locke employed it, and so recent a writer as McTaggart uses the terms " substance " and " attribute " in a manner that seems very like the traditional one. But in general in modern times we find in discussions relating to the nature and immortality of the soul a tendency to employ rather such terms as " personality," " self," and " personal identity." The content of these terms is variously described; but they are intended by most writers to designate the conscious self-identity that belongs to the individual. Yet this only pushes the difficulty one stage further on, for as Royce, agreeing essentially with Aristotle, points out, it is past man's power to define adequately what an individual really is: we may say that he is unique, that he is consciously purposeful, that his purpose has a meaning, that he belongs " not to this world of our merely human sense and thought," and that he is truly individual in relation " to other individuals and to the all inclusive Individual, God himself." Beyond this the idealist can hardly go.[110]

In this description, as in the expressions of most philosophers who regard the purposeful soul as something spiritual with the capacity of an endless life before it, we find much that is parallel to ancient views. With Plato, Aristotle, and the Stoics the human reason and will are made prime elements of the individual personality, expressive of that personality, and contributing to its growth and perfection — that is, the concept of the " self," the " soul," is dynamic not static. Again both ancient and modern thinkers agree in regarding the question of personality and its survival as one of value, and in holding that Goodness, Truth, and Beauty are realities because they have meaning in man's experience. Virtue is knowledge, taught Socrates, since by knowledge man has understanding of the unchanging principles on which progress toward perfection depends. Apprehension of these principles through reason and action in accord with them under the promptings of the will bring growth in wisdom and virtue alike. Hence Plato never separates his metaphysics and ethics, but binds them inextricably together. His world is teleological, as is that of Aristotle whose emphasis on final causes leaves no doubt of his position here. In modern discussions questions of value have occupied much attention and in idealistic circles especially have had much to do with religion. As has just been stated, Goodness, Truth, and Beauty are held to derive their meaning from conscious human experience: this experience is the measure of their value and thus provides the warrant of their reality; for as Plato held, the very essence of reality consists in value. Those who take this view today, however, deny against Plato that the Good, the Beautiful, and the True have a real existence apart from the conscious person, the individual; but they are at one with him in holding that they are realities in the experience of man and of God: in Him they are eternally and perfectly realized, as they are temporarily and partially in man.

The strongest argument for immortality today among those who do not put their chief trust in revelation is ethical and teleological. Those who use this argument do not claim for it the certainty that is secured in physical science, whose relative exactitude depends on physical measurements; but they justly point out that if such conclusive evidence be demanded everywhere, we must remain in deepest ignorance on most matters, and these often of the greatest importance to us, for physical measurement can be applied only to those facts that can be apprehended by the senses. The argument then must turn on constant human experience. On that basis it is maintained that the upright man's purposefulness which leads him to try to realize more perfectly in his own experience that which seems good, and his capacity to secure the good in ever greater realization are reasons for believing that an endless existence is before him; for it seems clear that man has in himself a capacity for growth that never is, and cannot be, exhausted in this life, and that in fact the perfection at which he aims is not to be secured in finite time. Therefore unless man's noblest aspirations, hopes, and efforts are to be mocked, unless indeed human existence is devoid of worth and meaning, man's spiritual life must continue without temporal limit beyond the grave.

Those who thus argue do not feel their position weakened by the fact that many men are not ambitious to realize their higher potentialities or that considerable numbers now seem unable to make the proper effort. The problem of the future state of such or of the obstinately wicked is not so promptly solved today as in the past. Some are in essential agreement with Origen in holding that in the mercy of God and through his love all will sometime be turned from their sins and ultimately find joy according to their capacity; others follow the traditional belief that the wicked in this world are doomed to endless punishment in the next although few thinking men can still picture the torments of the damned in the materialistic fashion in which the ancient Orphics and most teachers of the Christian Church down to our own times have painted them.[111] Apart from other considerations the concept of moral growth as a process of endless possibilities, and the loss of confidence in the efficacy of vindictive punishment or the justice of it, have had a profound influence on the speculations of even those who are most inclined to follow tradition. Therefore the majority of unbiased thinkers today are as disinclined to attempt the detailed portrayal of the fate of the morally unambitious or the wicked, as they are to describe the future happiness of the righteous. Yet many suggest another possibility: namely, that the wicked, having turned away from growth in virtue, which is held to be the essence of spiritual life, are doomed to death.[112]

The corollary of this view is the belief in "conditional immortality"; that is, that only those souls will live forever who by their capacity and will to grow toward perfection are fitted to survive. Stated thus the doctrine at first glance looks like a product of the past seventy years; yet it has an ancient, though often disregarded, lineage. Although Plato regarded the soul as naturally immortal, he did not commit himself to eschatological details, but like a poet resorted to myths to hint at truth. Nevertheless he recognized that men's escape from sin and their advance in virtue vary greatly; he held that only the true philosopher after three incarnations may escape from the weary round of death and life; in fact, he taught that only the soul that always loves Wisdom and seeks the Good can hope for eternal bliss. In other words, Plato's concept, like that of the modern was dynamic, and growth toward perfection was for him the sure warrant of immortality. Although he is not clear as to the ultimate fate of the obstinate sinner, logically he should have argued that the souls of the persistently wicked perish because of their sin. Such was the view expressed by Philo; and the same doctrine is found in the *First Epistle of Clement,* the *Didache,* and in the writings of the Gnostic Valentinus, as well as in the works of a number of the early fathers of the Church. Moreover it has always been possible for the Christian to appeal to Holy Writ, since Ezekiel had declared that " the soul that sinneth, it shall die," and the author of the *Epistle to the Romans* had written that " the wages of sin is death." [113]

There have been more recent theologians and philosophers who have held kindred views. In the sixteenth century Socinianism claimed that man is not naturally immortal; in the seventeenth Hobbes and Spinoza, in his early period, were inclined toward conditional immortality; so Locke and certain other English thinkers in the eighteenth; and during the last century and a half the number of significant thinkers on both sides of the Atlantic who by various paths have reached the conditional point of view is large. They maintain that the immortal life is the guerdon of him alone who by faith and righteous effort joins himself to God.[114]

There are two other doctrines which may be mentioned, although neither postulates the infinite existence of the conscious personality. One is that which is frequently called " corporate immortality " by which is meant that the influence of the individual on his fellows and his successors is permanent, that his aspirations, hopes, and deeds live in their effects on the race. It is hardly necessary to point out that while this doctrine may supply the individual with a powerful ethical motive, witness the Stoics and all their descendants, it has nothing to do with immortality of the conscious individual. The second also is akin to the views of the ancient Stoics and to pantheistic doctrines in general, for it holds that the human soul is a part of the Divine, or as Epictetus put it, "a splinter of God." Incorporate, it lives its life on earth, and at the dissolution of the body is reabsorbed in God, losing its sense of separateness, of individuality, but finding its satisfaction in reunion with the Divine. We have earlier noted that Greek thought laid comparatively little stress on the survival of the individual: Plato leaves the question unanswered, and the Neoplatonists are no more explicit; yet the conditions under which their Vision of God might be granted require the loss of the conscious self, and imply that in the final bliss of the faithful the individual is to be absorbed in the whole. The same is true in greater or less degree of all Christian concepts of the Beatific Vision. Yet over against this fact we must remember that most modern thinkers regard the unity of the world not as a mere sum total of individuals but as a whole in which each individual through his relations to all other individuals is inextricably bound to them; and yet he is not lost in the whole. This means that not only the Absolute includes all individuals, but also that the individuals may be self-conscious Persons; and if so, that such Persons may consciously survive through indefinite time, that the process of perfection may continue. Such and kindred views go beyond ancient and mediaeval thought in that they lay emphasis on the unbroken process of growth by which personality is developed.[115]

THIS survey, brief and fragmentary as it is, will suggest, we trust, how the stream of thought that today bears men's hopes, doubts, and firm beliefs concerning immortality, has its springs in ancient thinking. When we reason on this high theme, we are truly debtors both to the Greeks and to the Barbarians; both to the wise and to the unwise. Plato, Aristotle, Plotinus, Paul, Jesus, and many others unnamed and often now unknown, have made the succeeding generations their heirs.

NOTES AND BIBLIOGRAPHY

NOTES

1. That both tendance and worship of the dead were practised in the Aegean area during the second millenium B.C. seems probable. The evidence from Crete showing a care and reverence for the departed is abundant, but the proofs of actual worship are few: the chief Cretan monuments that may possibly show such worship are a painted sarcophagus from Hagia Triada, dating from Late Minoan II/III, and a painted larnax from Episcopi. Cf. M. P. Nilsson, *Minoan-Mycenaean Religion,* Lund, 1927, pp. 368–381, where a resumé of the various interpretations proposed may be found with references to all the significant literature. Nilsson himself sees on the sarcophagus from Hagia Triada evidence for the deification of the dead and for the worship of the new god with forms of the divine cult.

On the Greek mainland the proofs are more abundant. Ornaments, weapons, and other objects were buried with the dead in the shaft-graves at Mycenae; burnt offerings also were made there; and the graves were so arranged that libations might be poured down to the dead. There is also evidence that slaves were sacrificed to serve their noble masters (C. Tsountas and J. I. Manatt, *The Mycenaean Age,* Boston, 1897, pp. 87 ff., 312; R. Dussaud, *Les civilisations préhelléniques,*[2] Paris, 1914, pp. 398 ff.). Apparently offerings were made there as late as the sixth century B.C. (*IG.,* IV. 495); and before a beehive tomb at Menidi in Attica the tendance of the dead was continued down to the fifth century (A. Furtwängler and G. Löschcke, *Mykenische Vasen,* Berlin, 1886, pl. XI; P. Wolters, in *Jahrb. d. K. D. A. Inst.,* XIV, 1899, pp. 117 ff.). Cf. Axel W. Person, " Ein mykenisches Kenotaph in Dendrá," in *Arch. f. Religionswiss.,* XXVII, 1929, pp. 385–394. In many other places on the Greek mainland similar evidence has been discovered (P. Stengel, *Opferbräuche*, Leipzig, 1910, pp. 136 ff.; *Griech. Kultusaltertümer*,[3] München, 1920, pp. 144 ff., with references there given).

2. *Od.*, XI. 488 ff.

3. *Il.*, XXIII. 161–183; 217–221.

4. *Od.*, XI. 21 ff. The cenotaph built for one who died abroad may also be mentioned. Cf. R. K. Hack, "Homer and the Cult of Heroes," in *Trans. Am. Phil. Assn.*, LX. pp. 57–74 (1929).

5. Cf. P. Stengel, *Die Griechischen Kultusaltertümer*,[3] München, 1920, pp. 145 ff., and the references there given.

6. *Orph. frg.* 222, Kern; cf. Pindar, *Ol.*, II. 63 ff.

7. *Orph. frg.* 224b, Kern.

8. *Emped. frg.* 115, Diels.

9. *Orph. frg.* 32e, Kern.

10. Aristophanes, *Frogs*, 454 ff.; Andocides, *De Mys.*, 31.

11. According to Cicero, *Tusc. Disp.*, I. 16. 38, Pherecydes of Syros, who wrote in the middle of the sixth century B.C., was the first to express in writing a belief that men's souls are immortal: itaque credo equidem etiam alios tot saeculis, sed, quod litteris exstet, Pherecydes Syrius primum dixit animos esse hominum sempiternos. Cicero's comment, however, is much to the point: antiquus sane; fuit enim meo regnante gentili. Hanc opinionem discipulus eius Pythagoras maxime confirmavit; eqs.

12. *Phaedo*, 64–68, especially 64a: κινδυνεύουσι γὰρ ὅσοι τυγχάνουσιν ὀρθῶς ἁπτόμενοι φιλοσοφίας λεληθέναι τοὺς ἄλλους ὅτι οὐδὲν ἄλλο αὐτοὶ ἐπιτηδεύουσιν ἢ ἀποθνήσκειν τε καὶ τεθνάναι. εἰ οὖν τοῦτο ἀληθές, ἄτοπον δήπου ἂν εἴη προθυμεῖσθαι μὲν ἐν παντὶ τῷ βίῳ μηδὲν ἄλλο ἢ τοῦτο, ἥκοντος δὲ δὴ αὐτοῦ ἀγανακτεῖν, ὃ πάλαι προυθυμοῦντό τι καὶ ἐπετήδευον.

13. *Phaedo*, 70c–72d.

14. In the *Meno*, 81 ff., Socrates by his inquiries leads a slave to recognize that the square of the hypotenuse of an equilateral right-angle triangle is double the square of either of the sides — a truth which the slave must "recall," since no one has ever taught him it.

This doctrine of reminiscence is probably Pythagorean in its origin. It was apparently familiar to Cebes but not to Simmias, unless indeed Plato represented the latter as ignorant for dramatic purposes. Cf. A. E. Taylor, *Plato, The Man and his Work*, London, 1926, p. 186, n. 2.

15. *Phaedo*, 72E–77D.

16. Cf. *Rep.*, 608C–609; 621 B–D; *Laws*, 904–905B.

17. *Phaedrus*, 245C–246A; *Laws*, 893B–896D.

18. Yet the Neoplatonists regarded absorption into the Divine as the highest reward of the human soul.

19. *Phaedo*, 63 ff.; 66E ff.; 81 ff.; *Cratylus*, 399 f.; *Rep.*, 614 ff.; *Phaedrus*, 248B ff.

20. *Rep.*, 363; 612 f.; *Theaetetus*, 176–177A.

21. *De anima*, 415a, 23 ff. ἡ γὰρ θρεπτικὴ ψυχὴ καὶ τοῖς ἄλλοις ὑπάρχει, καὶ πρώτη καὶ κοινοτάτη δύναμίς ἐστι ψυχῆς, καθ' ἣν ὑπάρχει τὸ ζῆν ἅπασιν. Cf. 414a, 29 ff.; 429a, 10 ff.; 430a, 22 ff.

22. *De anima*, 413b, 14 ff.; 429a, 22 ff. Cf. *De gen. anim.*, 736b, 27: λείπεται τὸν νοῦν μόνον θύραθεν ἐπεισιέναι καὶ θεῖον εἶναι μόνον.

23. Cf. *De anima*, 430a, 22 ff. with Simplicius's commentary thereto, and Themist., 99, 24 f. (Heinze); *Meta.*, 1072a, 30 ff.

24. Diog. Laert., VII. 134 = *SVF.*, II. 300; Seneca, *Epist.*, 65.2 = *SVF.*, II. 303.

25. Epict., *Diss.*, I. 14. 6; II. 8. 11.

26. Epicur., *frg.* 311Us.; Diog. Laert., X. 63 ff.; Lucretius, III. 418 ff.

27. Plut., *De sera num. vind.*, 16–18; Philo, *De post. Cain.*, 43; *De somn.*, I. 149.

28. Plot., *Enn.*, IV. 2. 1. p. 363: ἡ δ'ὁμοῦ μεριστή τε καὶ ἀμέριστος φύσις, ἣν δὴ ψυχὴν εἶναί φαμεν, οὐχ οὕτως ὡς τὸ συνεχὲς μία, μέρος ἄλλο, τὸ δ'ἄλλο ἔχουσα, ἀλλὰ μεριστὴ μέν, ὅτι ἐν πᾶσι μέρεσι τοῦ ἐν ᾧ ἐστιν, ἀμέριστος δέ, ὅτι ὅλη ἐν πᾶσι καὶ ἐν ὁτῳοῦν αὐτῶν ὅλη. The apparent contradiction here is probably due to Plato's *Timaeus* (35A), where between the divisible and indivisible a third category is placed in which the two former are combined. Both thinkers were wrestling with the difficulty of admitting unity and multiplicity without difference in essence.

29. Plot., *Enn.*, V. 1 *et passim;* cf. Porph., *Vita Plot.*, 1 ff.; *ad Marc.* 32; *de Abst.*, I. 31.

30. Plot., *Enn.*, V. 9. 1; I. 2.

31. Plot., *Enn.*, VI. 9. 3–11; Porph., *Vita Plot.*, 23.

32. Plot., *Enn.*, IV. 7; VI. 4. 16; cf. III. 2. 4; IV. 8. 4.

33. *Ibid.*, I. 6. 6; III. 4. 6; IV. 3. 24.

34. Cf. Cicero, *de leg.*, II. 36.

35. See the whole series of inscriptions, *C.I.L.*, VI. 497–504. The worship of Isis had spread to southern Italy as early as the second century B.C.; by the middle of the next century it was popular at Rome and in many parts of the western provinces, and the cult had a strong hold during the first three centuries of our era over wide areas. But the mysteries of Mithras were the most popular during the first two and a half Christian centuries. After about A.D. 250 the evidence for the rites of all these Oriental cults, and of all pagan cults in general, outside the city of Rome, becomes increasingly rare. Cf. F. Cumont, *Oriental Religions in Roman Paganism,* Chicago, 1911; J. F. Toutain, *Les cultes païens dans l'empire romain,* Paris, 1906–17, II; C. H. Moore, "The Pagan Reaction in the Late Fourth Century," in *Transactions of Am. Phil. Ass'n,* L, 122 ff. (1919).

36. *Job*, XIV. 7–12.

37. *Id.*, XIV. 14. Cf. XX. 7.

38. *Id.*, XIX. 25–27.

39. *Is.*, XXIV–XXVII.

40. *Dan.*, VII–XII; *Wisdom of Solomon*, II–III; cf. *Ecclesiasticus.*

41. On the whole subject of the Jewish concepts of the hereafter, see G. F. Moore, *Judaism,* Cambridge, Harv. Univ. Press, 1927, II, Part VII, pp. 279–395.

42. Cf. *Rom.*, VII. 7–25. Apparently Paul used νοῦς as equivalent to πνεῦμα, and in *Rom.*, VII. 18–25 we find not only νοῦς but τὸ θέλειν τὸ καλόν, ἔσω ἄνθρωπος, and ὁ νόμος τοῦ νοός used as virtually equivalent.

43. The argument from silence in this epistle obviously

must not be pushed too far, for the future life is not the chief subject that the author is discussing.

44. Clement, I. 24–26; cf. II Clement 20; Ignatius, *ad Smyr.* 5 f.; *Didache* 16; Barnabas 5; cf. Polycarp, *ad Phil.* 2; Justin, *Apol.* I. 18 f.; II. 9; Athenagoras, *De resurrectione, passim,* esp. 13 ff. Athenagoras is obviously moved by the view that man's personality depends on the two factors, soul and body; and he does not share the common dualistic belief of the Orphics and Platonists that body and soul are opposed by nature. Cf. *ibid.* 20 and 25.

45. *Ad Aut.* II, 27: εἰ γὰρ ἀθάνατον αὐτὸν ἀπ' ἀρχῆς πεποιήκει, θεὸν αὐτὸν πεποιήκει· πάλιν εἰ θνητὸν αὐτὸν πεποιήκει, ἐδόκει ἂν ὁ θεὸς αἴτιος εἶναι τοῦ θανάτου αὐτοῦ. Οὔτε οὖν ἀθάνατον αὐτὸν ἐποίησεν οὔτε μὴν θνητόν, ἀλλὰ καθὼς ἐπάνω προειρήκαμεν, δεκτικὸν ἀμφοτέρων, ἵνα, εἰ ῥέψῃ ἐπὶ τὰ τῆς ἀθανασίας τηρήσας τὴν ἐντολὴν τοῦ θεοῦ, μισθὸν κομίσηται παρ' αὐτοῦ τὴν ἀθανασίαν καὶ γένηται θεός, εἰ δ' αὖ τραπῇ ἐπὶ τὰ τοῦ θανάτου πράγματα παρακούσας τοῦ θεοῦ, αὐτὸς ἑαυτῷ αἴτιος ᾖ τοῦ θανάτου. Cf. Tatian 13.

46. Tertullian, *De anima* and *De resur. carnis, passim.*

47. Irenaeus, *Contra Her.,* especially III. 18–23; V, *praef.,* 16; Hippol., *Refutat.,* X. 32–34 W.

48. Irenaeus, V., *passim.* Like Tertullian, Hippolytus, and others, Irenaeus rejected chiliasm and held that six thousand years of the world's history must elapse before Christ should return to destroy the Antichrist and reign with the saints.

49. *Refut.,* X. 34. 4: γέγονας γὰρ θεός· ὅσα γὰρ ὑπέμεινας πάθη ἄνθρωπος ὤν, ταῦτα ἐδίδου ὅτι ἄνθρωπος εἶς, ὅσα δὲ παρακολουθεῖ θεῷ, ταῦτα παρέχειν ἐπήγγελται θεός, ὅταν θεοποιηθῇς, ἀθάνατος γεννηθείς. For such a view support would be found in the Pauline writings, especially in the *Epistle to the Ephesians.*

50. *Symposium:* Diotima's speech as reported by Socrates, especially 211d–212a; *Rep.,* VI. 504 ff., et *passim.*

51. *Gal.,* I. 11–12; *Eph.,* III. 3–4.

52. Irenaeus, *Contra. Haer.,* I. 5–8.

53. Irenaeus, *Contra. Haer.,* II. 48: esse autem resurrectionem a mortuis agnitionem eius quae ab eis dicitur veritatis. Cf. Tertullian, *De carnis resur.,* 19: resurrectionem

quoque mortuorum manifeste annuntiatam in imaginariam significationem distorquent, asseverantes ipsam etiam mortem spiritaliter intelligendam. Non enim hanc esse in vero, . . . , discidium carnis atque animae, sed ignorantiam dei, per quam homo mortuus deo, non minus in errore iacuerit quam in sepulchro. Itaque et resurrectionem eam vindicandam, qua quis adita veritate redanimatus et revivificatus deo, ignorantiae morte discussa, velut de sepulchro veteris hominis eruperit.

54. Cf. H. L. Mansel, *The Gnostic Heresies in the First and Second Centuries*, London, 1875; E. de Faye, *Gnostiques et Gnosticisme*,[2] Paris, 1925; A. Harnack, *History of Dogma*, I. pp. 222–265; II, *passim*.

55. Note the significant full title of the *Stromateis*: τῶν κατὰ τὴν ἀληθῆ φιλοσοφίαν γνωστικῶν ὑπομνημάτων στρωματεῖς.

56. *Strom.*, II. 12; VII, entire.

57. On the human soul, see Origen, *De prin.*, II. 8. 10, 7; III. 1 and 4; IV. 1. 36; Clement, *Paed.*, III. 1. 1; cf. Plato, *Rep.*, IV. 436a–441c; *Tim.*, 69a–72d. On the revelation of the Logos and the redemptive death of Christ, see Origen, *C. Cels.*, VII. 17; cf. I. 31; *Exhort. ad Mart.*, entire.

58. Origen, *C. Cels.*, III. 59–62; VI. 68; VII. 46. Cf. *In Ioh.*, I. 20–22.

59. *De prin.*, I. 6; II. 3. 10. 11; III. 6. 4 ff.; *Sel. in Psal.*, I. 5; *C. Cels.*, V. 22 ff.

60. *De prin.*, III. 1. 21: possibile est ut vel a summo bono ad infima mala discendat (anima), vel ab ultimis malis ad summa bona reparetur. Cf. *ibid.*, I. 6. 3. Yet Origen expressly denies that the soul can fall past all recovery in future life. *In Rom.*, V. 10. Also *De prin.*, II. 11. 4 ff. Cf. *C. Cels.*, V. 15; *In Luc. Hom.*, XIV.

61. Cf. Jerome's criticism, *Ad Avitum* (*Ep.* CXXIV).

62. Likewise the Mithraists. F. Cumont, *Mystères de Mithra*, Paris, 1902, pp. 119 f., Eng. trans., pp. 144 f., Chicago, 1903; id., *After Life in Roman Paganism*, chs. III, VI, and VII., *passim*, New Haven, 1922.

63. Clement, *Strom.*, IV. 25; VI. 14; VII. 10.

64. Origen, *C. Cels.*, VI. 21; *De prin.*, II. 11.

65. It must be said that Origen nowhere sets forth these views as systematic doctrine, but his belief can be gathered from the following passages: *In Num.*, XXI. 1; XXVIII. 2–4. *In Math. Comm. Series*, 39. Jerome (*Ep.* LXXXIV, Migne) unjustly charged that Origen taught that Gabriel and the Devil would attain the same good in the end.

66. The ethical arguments of Methodius, however, and his view of the human soul as material show in part the persistent influence of Stoic doctrines. Cf. E. Buonaiuti, " The Ethics and the Eschatology of Methodius of Olympus," in *Harvard Theol. Rev.*, XIV. pp. 255 ff. (1921).

67. Cf. T. L. Shear, *The Influence of Plato on St. Basil*, Baltimore, 1906; C. Gronau, *De Basilio, Gregorio Nazianzeno Nyssenoque Platonis imitatoribus*, Göttingen, 1908; Geffcken, *Kynika und Verwandtes*, Heidelberg, 1909, pp. 18 ff.; Büttner, *Beiträge zur Ethik Basileios des Grossen*, Landshut, 1913; Pinault, *Le platonisme de St. Gregoire de Nazianze*, La Roch-sur-Yon Romain, 1925; H. F. Cherniss, *The Platonism of Gregory of Nyssa*, Berkeley, Calif., 1930.

68. Nos. 27–31, of A.D. 380.

69. *De an. et resur.*, PG. XLVI, 49 BC and 64 AB: ἐπεὶ δὲ τοῖς μὲν τὰς τεχνικὰς ἐφόδους μεμελετηκόσι τῶν ἀποδείξεων, ὁ συλλογισμὸς ἱκανὸς εἰς πίστιν δοκεῖ · ἡμῖν δὲ πάντων τῶν τεχνικῶν συμπερασμάτων ἕξις πιστότερον εἶναι ὡμολογεῖται τὸ διὰ τῶν ἱερῶν τῆς Γραφῆς διδαγμάτων ἀναφαινόμενον· ζητεῖν οἶμαι δεῖν ἐπὶ τοῖς εἰρημένοις, εἰ ἡ θεόπνευστος διδασκαλία τούτοις συμφέρεται. Cf. 'Α. Μ. "Ακυλας, Ἡ περὶ ἀθανασίας τῆς ψυχῆς δόξα τοῦ Πλάτωνος ἐν συγκρίσει πρὸς τὴν Γρηγορίου τοῦ Νύσσης, Athens, 1888; K. Gronau, *Poseidonius und die jüdisch-christliche Genesisexegese*, Leipzig, 1914.

70. *Contra Eunomium*, PG. XLV, 545A ff.; cf. *In cant. cant.*, PG. XLIV, 777D ff.; *de an. et resur.*, PG. XLVI, 17A ff.

71. *De an. et resur.*, PG. XLVI, 100C ff.; 148A.

72. *De hom. opif.* 16, PG. XLIV, 177D ff.

73. *De beat.* VI, PG. XLIV, 1269C ff., 1272A ff.

74. *De vita Moysis*, PG. XLIV, 376D f.; cf. H. Koch, in *Theol. Quartalsch.*, LXXX. pp. 397 ff. (1898).

75. The controversies over the identity of Macarius and concerning the writings that pass under his name do not here concern us. (Cf. Christ-Schmidt, *Griech. Litteraturgeschichte*,⁶ II. 2. 1386). But the influence of the works attributed to him is beyond question. It is improbable that Macarius was directly affected by Stoic doctrine to the extent claimed by J. Stoffels, "Makarius der Aegypter auf den Faden der Stoa," in *Theol. Quartalsch.*, XCII. pp. 88 ff., 243 ff. (1910). His views are rather based directly on the Bible, not least of all on the Pauline writings; and for the most part they accord with views current in his time. He differs from his predecessors and contemporaries chiefly in emphasis.

76. *PG.* XXXIV, 457B, 480 A–C, 893C ff. 496C, 621B ff., 648C ff.

77. *Ibid.*, XXXIV, 913C: τὰ εἰρημένα ταυτὶ τοῦ Πνεύματος ἐνεργήματα, μεγάλων μέτρων εἰσί, καὶ τῶν ἐγγυτάτω τῆς τελειότητος· Αὖται γὰρ αἱ ποικίλαι τῆς χάριτος παρακλήσεις διαφόρως μὲν, ἀλλ' ἀδιαλείπτως αὐτοῖς ἀπὸ τοῦ Πνεύματος ἐνεργοῦνται, ἐνεργείας ἐνέργειαν πνεύματος διαδεχομένης. Ὁπότε γὰρ εἰς τὴν τελειότητά τις τοῦ Πνεύματος καταντήσειε, πάντων ἀκριβῶς τῶν πάθων ἀποκαθαρθείς, καὶ ὅλως τῷ Παρακλήτῳ Πνεύματι διὰ τῆς ἀρρήτου κοινωνίας ἐνωθείς· ἐπειδὰν καὶ αὐτὴ ἡ ψυχὴ καταξιωθείη Πνεῦμα γενέσθαι, ὡς συγκραθεῖσα τῷ Πνεύματι τότε ὅλον φῶς, ὅλον χάρα, ὅλον ἀνάπαυσις, ὅλον ἀγαλλίασις, ὅλον ἀγάπη, ὅλον σπλάγχνα, ὅλον ἀγαθότης, καὶ χρηστότης γίνεται· κτλ. Cf. also the entire treatise *De caritate*.

78. *Ibid.*, XXXIV, 745A: Ἐν δὲ τῇ ἀναστάσει τῶν σωμάτων ὧν προανέστησαν καὶ προεδοξάσθησαν αἱ ψυχαὶ τότε καὶ τὰ σώματα συνδοξάζονται καὶ φωτίζονται τῇ ἀπὸ τοῦ νῦν πεφωτισμένῃ καὶ δεδοξασμένῃ ψυχῇ· ἔστι γὰρ αὐτῶν οἶκος καὶ σκηνὴ καὶ πόλις ὁ Κύριος.

749A: Ἀνάστασις τῶν νεκρῶν ψυχῶν ἀπὸ τοῦ νῦν γίνεται. Ἀνάστασις δὲ τῶν σωμάτων ἐν ἐκείνῃ τῇ ἡμέρᾳ. Cf. 581C.

79. *De div. nom., passim*, esp. I and XIII: *PG.* III, 585B ff., 977B ff.; cf. 888B.

80. *De mys. theol., passim*: *PG.* III, 997A ff. Cf. St. John XVII, 3.

81. *De div. nom.*, II. 4. 11; IX. 9: *PG.* III, 640D ff.,

649B ff., 916CD. Cf. *De mys. theol.* II, III: *PG.* III, 1025 ff.; cf. Proclus, *in Tim. Plat.*, 211 B and scholia thereto (Vol. I, p. 468 Diehl).

82. *De div. nom.*, IV. 18 ff.: *PG.* III, 715D ff.

83. The treatises *de coel. hier.* and *de eccl. hier.* should be consulted entire for a full understanding of these matters which can only be touched on here.

84. *De mys. theol.*, I. 3: *PG.* III. 1000C ff.: πᾶς ὢν τοῦ πάντων ἐπέκεινα, καὶ οὐδενὸς οὔτε ἑαυτοῦ οὔτε ἑτέρου, τῷ παντελῶς δὲ ἀγνώστῳ τῆς πάσης γνώσεως ἀνενεργησίᾳ, κατὰ τὸ κρεῖττον ἑνούμενος, καὶ τῷ μηδὲν γινώσκειν, ὑπὲρ νοῦν γινώσκων. *De div. nom.*, IV. 13: *PG.* III, 712A f., where Dionysius supports his argument by quoting Paul, *Gal.*, II. 20: ζῶ δέ, οὐκ ἔτι ἐγώ, ζῇ δὲ ἐν ἐμοὶ Χριστός.

85. *De div. nom.*, VIII. 9: *PG.* III, 897A f.; *Epist.*, IV: *PG.* III, 1072A ff.; cf. *ibid.*, 1108A f.

86. Étienne H. Gilson, *Introduction à l'étude de Saint-Augustin*, Paris, 1929, is one of the latest and best books on Augustine's doctrines. It contains, pp. 309–331, a bibliography of the principal works relating to Augustine and his philosophy down to 1927 inclusive.

87. *Solil.*, I. 2. 7: Deum et animam scire cupio. Nihilne plus? Nihil omnino. *Ibid.*, I. 15. 27: Animam te certe dicis et deum velle cognoscere? Hoc est totum negotium meum. Nihilne amplius? Nihil prorsus. *Ibid.*, II. 1: Noverim me, noverim te. *Epist.*, CXVIII. 3. 13 ff.; *De trin.*, VIII. 3. 4 f.; *Conf.*, V. 4; X. 17 ff.; *De civ. dei*, X. 6; *De Gen. ad litt.*, VII. 28: Nunc tamen de anima quam deus inspiravit homini sufflando in eius faciem, nihil confirmo, nisi quia ex deo sic est, ut non sit substantia dei; et sit incorporea, id est, non sit corpus, sed spiritus; cf. *De trin.*, X. 5 ff. 10; *Epist.*, CXXXVII. 3. 11.

In Augustine's psychology, it is true that he recognizes a superior part and inferior part of the soul. For the soul as a whole, like most of his predecessors, he employs the general terms *anima* and *animus* without distinction; the superior part, which is the intelligence (*mens, ratio*), he names *spiritus* or *animus* in this narrower sense. The inferior, which includes the senses and vital force, he distinguishes by *anima*. (*De trin.*, XV. 1. 1; *De anima et eius orig.*, IV. 22 f.)

88. *De quant. an.*, XIII. 22; *De civ. dei*, I. 13; X. 29; *De anima et eius orig.*, II. 2 f.; IV. 2; *Epist.*, CXXXVII. 3. 11; cf. *De quant. an.*, I. 32. 69; *De mor. eccl. cath.*, I. 27. 52.

89. *De trin.*, XIII. 9: Fides autem ista totum hominem futurum, qui utique constat ex anima et corpore; et ob hoc beatum, non argumentatione humana sed divina auctoritate promittit.

90. Plotinus's arguments for the immortality of the soul are virtually all given in *Enn.*, IV. 7.

91. *De Gen. ad litt.*, X. 1 ff.; cf. *De civ. dei*, X. 31.

92. *Solil.*, II. 12–19.

93. Plot., *Enn.*, VII. 3; Aug., *De immort.*, 5 ff.

94. *De trin.*, XIII. 8; cf. *ibid.* 3; also *De civ. dei*, X. 1; XI. 27.

95. *De trin.*, XIII. 9.

96. On original sin, grace, etc., see especially the following works: *De libero arbitrio PL.* XXXII, 1221 ff.; *De diversis quaest. ad Simplicianum* XL, 102 ff.; *De gratia Christi et de peccato originali* XLIV, 359 ff.; *De gratia et libero arbitrio, ibid.*, 881 ff.; *De correptione et gratia, ibid.*, 915 ff.; *De praedestione sanctorum, ibid.*, 959 ff.; *De dono perseverantiae, ibid.*, 993 ff.

On the fate of the soul after death, consult: *De Gen. ad litt.*, VIII. 5; XII. 32 ff.; *De civ. dei*, XIX. 27 f.; XXI. 10; XXII. 29 f.

97. See Ueberweg-Geyer, *Grundriss d. Gesch. d. Phil.*, 11te Aufl., Berlin, 1928, II, pp. 743 ff. for a full bibliography on the life and works of St. Thomas. For a selected bibliography consult Maurice De Wulf, *Histoire de la philosophie médiévale*, 5me ed., Louvain, 1925, II, pp. 30 ff.

98. See Prol. to *S. Theol.*, I. q. 1, 1–8. and *S. c. gent.*, I. 4–8.

99. *Com. ad Arist. de anima*, III. 8 (431b, 21 ff.) lect. 13: intellectus est quaedam potentia receptiva omnium formarum intelligibilium et sensus est quaedam potentia receptiva omnium formarum sensibilium; *S. Theol.*; I, qq.

NOTES

84–89. Cf. N. Kaufmann, " Die Erkenntnisslehre des hl. Thomas," in *Philos. Jahrb.*, II. 22 ff. (1889). A. Schneider, " Der Gedanke der Erkenntniss des Gleichen durch Gleiches in antiker und patristischer Zeit," in *Festschrift für Cl. Baeumker*, Beiträge, Suppl. II. 65 ff. (1923).

100. Prol. to *S. Theol.*, I q. 1.; 2, a. 1. Cf. Augustine's *credo ut intelligam;* also William James, *The Will to Believe,* for a forceful modern application of an ancient principle.

101. *S. Theol.*, I. q. 2, a. 2–3; *S. c. gent.*, I, c. 13. The five proofs are in brief as follows: (1) the fact that movement and change demand that we postulate an immovable mover; otherwise we must suppose that the series of movers and of objects moved is infinite, which would be equivalent to denying all real motion or change; (2) from the chain of causation that we observe everywhere, we must postulate a higher cause which operates on the lower causes; otherwise we are forced to believe here in an infinite chain, which would be to deny all genuine causation; (3) the distinction between the possible and the necessary: since the possible depends on the necessary, while the necessary depends on another necessary being or on itself, therefore we must postulate either an endless series, which is impossible, or a necessary independent being, which is the cause of all other necessary and contingent beings; (4) since Being, Goodness, Truth, and similar perfections are found in varying degrees in finite and limited beings, there must be some supreme and perfect Being which possesses these qualities in their perfection and in which all others share; (5) we see about us creatures which, although possessing no knowledge, still work toward an end which is best; therefore we are forced to believe that such creatures are guided by an intelligent Being.

While these proofs mainly go back to Aristotle, Thomas naturally was indebted to many thinkers nearer himself in time, chiefly Albertus Magnus, Avicenna, and Maimonides.

102. On the existence, nature, and power of God see especially *S. Theol.*, I. qq. 1–44; *S. c. gent.*, I entire; cf.

De ente et essentia, passim. On creation, see *S. Theol.,* I. 45–74; *S. c. gent.,* II. 1–38; III. 65.

103. *S. Theol.,* I. q. 4. 1: Primum autem principium materiale imperfectissimum est. Cum enim materia, in quantum hujusmodi sit in potentia, oportet quod primum principium materiale sit maxime in potentia et ita maxime imperfectum. Also *De ente et essentia,* 2: Materia non quolibet modo accepta est individuationis principium, sed solum matéria signata. Et dico materiam signatam quae sub determinatis dimensionibus consideratur. Cf. Aristotle, Metaph,. I. 6. 988a. 3.

104. *S. Theol.,* I. q. 12; I–II. *passim; S. c. gent.,* III. 24–63; 147–163.

105. *S. c. gent.,* IV. 27–78.

106. *Ibid.,* IV. 79–97.

107. See P. H. Wicksteed, *Dante and Aquinas,* London and New York, 1913; E. Bullough, *Dante, the Poet of St. Thomas,* Cambridge, Eng., 1925.

108. Consult Bernard's four works: *De consideratione, De gradibus humilitatis et superbiae, De diligendo deo, De gratia et libero arbitrio,* and the *Sermones in cantica canticorum, PL.* 182, 183, for his views. He was influenced primarily by Augustine, the *Song of Songs,* and the Pauline and Johannine writings of the *New Testament.* Bonaventura's mysticism appears most clearly in his *Itinerarium mentis in deum,* V. pp. 293 ff. in Quaracchi edition.

109. For a convenient presentation of modern Roman Catholic psychological views, consult the able *Psychology* [6] of Professor Michael Maher, S. J., New York, Longmans, 1909, from which (p. 461) my quotation is taken.

110. Cf. McTaggart, *Studies in Hegelian Cosmology,* pp. 41 ff.; A. Seth Pringle-Pattison, *The Idea of Immortality,* 1922, pp. 123 ff., 168 ff. for criticism of McTaggart's views; and pp. 62 ff. for a discussion of the relation of mind and body; Royce, *The Conception of Immortality,* Ingersoll Lecture, 1900, from which (pp. 73, 80) I quote.

Pringle-Pattison, *op. cit.,* p. 105, puts the matter clearly: " It is only the self-conscious spirit — a being who can make himself his own object and contemplate himself as a self —

that attains individuality and independence in an ultimate sense."

There are, however, weighty authorities opposed to such concepts: Spinoza, for example, regarded personality as an unreal appearance, and in our own time Bradley and Bosanquet have taken very much the same view. Yet it seems to many that such a conclusion fails to take into account man's consciousness of himself as an individual and an agent — which consciousness may be held to be a primary fact of experience, if conscious experience have any significance whatever.

111. Jonathan Edwards, on his severer side, will serve as a horrible example from recent times.

112. Compare Dante, *Inferno,* III. 34 ff.:

> *Questo misero modo*
> *Tengon l'anime triste di coloro*
> *Chè visser senza infamia e senza lodo.*

> *Mischiate sono a quel cattivo coro*
> *Degli angeli che non furon ribelli,*
> *Nè fur fedeli a Dio, ma per sè foro.*

> *Cacciarli i ciel per non esser men belli;*
> *Nè lo profondo Inferno li riceve,*
> *Chè alcuna gloria i rei avrebber d'elli.*

113. *Ez.,* XVIII. 4. 20; *Rom.,* VI. 23. It is true that the interpretation of these texts may be a matter for dispute, and that other texts could be quoted in opposition; but such facts have seldom deterred those who put their trust in proof texts. See " Conditional Immortality " in Hasting's *Encyclopaedia of Religion and Ethics.*

114. Cf. Pringle-Pattison, *op. cit.,* pp. 95 ff.; and Pètavel-Olliff, *Le problème de l'immortalité,* Paris, 1892, *passim,* and in particular I, pp. 15 ff.; 240 ff.

115. Cf. the works by Royce, McTaggart, and Pringle-Pattison referred to above.

BIBLIOGRAPHY

BESIDES the articles on *Immortality, Future Life, Conditional Immortality, Soul*, etc., in Hasting's *Encyclopaedia of Religion and Ethics; The Catholic Encyclopedia; Encyclopaedia Britannica*, and similar works, and the standard histories of philosophy, ancient, medieval, and modern, the following selected titles will be found useful:

BEET, J. A.
  The Immortality of the Soul. London, 1901.
BEVAN, EDWYN
  The Hope of a World to Come Underlying Judaism and Christianity. London, 1930.
BIGG, CHARLES
  The Christian Platonists of Alexandria. Oxford, 1886.
BOSANQUET, BERNARD
  The Principle of Individuality and Value. London, 1912.
  The True Conception of Another World, in " Essays and Addresses." London, 1891.
  The Value and Destiny of the Individual. London, 1913.
BRADLEY, F. H.
  Appearance and Reality.[2] London, 1897.
BURNET, JOHN
  The Socratic Doctrine of the Soul, in " Essays and Addresses." London, 1929.
CAIRD, JOHN
  Fundamental Ideas of Christianity. Glasgow, 1899.

BIBLIOGRAPHY

CARPENTER, J. E.
    The Place of Immortality in Religious Belief. London, 1898.

COURDAVEAUX, VICTOR
    De L'immortalité de L'âme dans le Stoicisme. Paris, 1857.

CUMONT, FRANZ
    After Life in Roman Paganism. New Haven, 1922.
    Les religions orientales dans le paganisme romain. 4me éd. Paris, 1929.
    English translation from the second French edition, *Oriental Religions in Roman Paganism.* Chicago, 1911.

DICKINSON, G. L.
    Religion and Immortality. London, 1911.

EVERETT, C. C.
    Theism and the Christian Hope, Chap. XXXIV. New York, 1909.

FALCONER, SIR ROBERT ALEXANDER
    The Idea of Immortality and Western Civilization. Cambridge, Harvard University Press, 1930.

FARNELL, L. R.
    Greek Hero Cults and Ideas of Immortality. Oxford, 1921.

FENN, WILLIAM WALLACE
    Immortality and Theism. Cambridge, Harvard University Press, 1921.

FISKE, JOHN
    The Destiny of Man. Boston, 1884.
    Through Nature to God. Boston, 1899.
    Life Everlasting. Boston, 1901.

GAYE, R. K.
    The Platonic Conception of Immortality and its Connection with the Theory of Ideas. London, 1904.

GILSON, ÉTIENNE
    Le Thomisme. Strasbourg, 1922.
    The Philosophy of St. Thomas Aquinas (Eng. trans.). Cambridge, England, 1929.

GORDON, G. A.
   Immortality and the New Theodicy. Boston, 1897.
HARNACK, ADOLPH
   Lehrbuch der Dogmengeschichte, 3 vols. 3d ed. Leipzig, 1894–97.
   English translation from the third German edition, *History of Dogma,* 7 vols. London, 1897–99.
HOCKING, W. E.
   The Self: Its Body and Freedom. New Haven, 1928.
VON HÜGEL, F.
   Eternal Life. Edinburgh, 1912.
JAMES, WILLIAM
   Two Supposed Objections to the Doctrine of Human Immortality. Boston, 1897.
KRÜGER, GUSTAV
   The Immortality of Man. Cambridge, Harvard University Press, 1927.
LAKE, KIRSOPP
   Immortality and the Modern Mind. Cambridge, Harvard University Press, 1922.
LYMAN, EUGENE W.
   The Meaning of Selfhood and Faith in Immortality. Cambridge, Harvard University Press, 1928.
McTAGGART, J. M. E.
   Studies in Hegelian Cosmology. Cambridge, England, 1901.
MACKENZIE, WILLIAM DOUGLAS
   Man's Consciousness of Immortality. Cambridge, Harvard University Press, 1929.
MATTHEWS, W. R. (editor)
   King's College Lectures on Immortality by J. F. Bethune-Baker and others. London, 1920.
MELLONE, S. H.
   The Immortal Hope. London, 1910.
MOORE, CLIFFORD H.
   Pagan Ideas of Immortality during the Early Roman Empire. Cambridge, Harvard University Press, 1918.

BIBLIOGRAPHY

MOORE, GEORGE F.
    Metempsychosis.   Cambridge,   Harvard   University
    Press, 1914.
OSTWALD, WILHELM
    Individuality and Immortality.   Boston, 1906.
OZANAM, ANTOINE FRÉDÉRIC
    Dante et la Philosophie Catholique au Troisième Siécle.
    Paris, 1839.
    English translation, New York, 1897.
PETAVEL–OLLIFF, EMMANUEL
    Le Problème de L'immortalité.   2 vols.   Paris, 1891,
    1892.
    English translation: *The Problem of Immortality*.
    London, 1892.
ROHDE, ERWIN
    Psyche. 2 vols. 7th and 8th edition, Tübingen, 1921.
    English Translation: *Psyche*. London and New York,
    1925.
ROYCE, JOSIAH
    The Conception of Immortality.   Boston, 1900.
    The World and the Individual (Gifford Lectures), 2d
    ser. London, 1901. Lect. VI, VII, X.
SETH PRINGLE–PATTISON, A.
    The Idea of Immortality (Gifford Lectures).   Oxford,
    1922.
    Man's Place in the Cosmos. London, 1902. (Espe-
    cially Essay I)
STOCKS, J. L.
    Aristotelianism (in " Our Debt to Greece and Rome "
    Series).   New York, 1925.
TAYLOR, A. E.
    Platonism and its Influence (in " Our Debt to Greece
    and Rome " Series).   New York, 1924.
    The Faith of a Moralist (Gifford Lectures, 1926–28).
    2 vols.   London, 1930.
TSANOFF, RADOSLAV A.
    The Problem of Immortality.   New York, 1924.

THE IMMORTALITY OF THE SOUL

TYLOR, E. B.
    Primitive Culture.[6] London, 1920. Chapters XI to
    XIV on the Soul.
WARD, J.
    The Realm of Ends. London, 1911. Lect's XVIII and
    XIX.
WELLDON, J. E. C.
    The Hope of Immortality. London, 1898.
WENLEY, R. M.
    Stoicism and its Influence (in " Our Debt to Greece
    and Rome " Series). New York, 1924.
WICKSTEED, PHILIP H.
    Dante and Aquinas. London and Toronto, 1913.

Our Debt to Greece and Rome

AUTHORS AND TITLES

AUTHORS AND TITLES

AESCHYLUS AND SOPHOCLES. *J. T. Sheppard.*

GREEK RELIGION. *Walter Woodburn Hyde.*

SURVIVALS OF ROMAN RELIGION. *Gordon J. Laing.*

MYTHOLOGY. *Jane Ellen Harrison.*

ANCIENT BELIEFS IN THE IMMORTALITY OF THE SOUL. *Clifford H. Moore.*

STAGE ANTIQUITIES. *James Turney Allen.*

PLAUTUS AND TERENCE. *Gilbert Norwood.*

ROMAN POLITICS. *Frank Frost Abbott.*

PSYCHOLOGY, ANCIENT AND MODERN. *G. S. Brett.*

ANCIENT AND MODERN ROME. *Rodolfo Lanciani.*

WARFARE BY LAND AND SEA. *Eugene S. McCartney.*

THE GREEK FATHERS. *James Marshall Campbell.*

GREEK BIOLOGY AND MEDICINE. *Henry Osborn Taylor.*

MATHEMATICS. *David Eugene Smith.*

LOVE OF NATURE AMONG THE GREEKS AND ROMANS. *H. R. Fairclough.*

ANCIENT WRITING AND ITS INFLUENCE. *B. L. Ullman.*

GREEK ART. *Arthur Fairbanks.*

ARCHITECTURE. *Alfred M. Brooks.*

ENGINEERING. *Alexander P. Gest.*

MODERN TRAITS IN OLD GREEK LIFE. *Charles Burton Gulick.*

ROMAN PRIVATE LIFE. *Walton Brooks McDaniel.*

GREEK AND ROMAN FOLKLORE. *William Reginald Halliday.*

ANCIENT EDUCATION. *J. F. Dobson.*